Slightly Bruised and a Little Broken

God Can Transform Tragedies into Triumphs

He has sent me to heal the brokenhearted (Isaiah 61:1)

Ephesians 4:22-23 "Strip yourselves of your former nature... And be constantly renewed in the spirit of your mind (having a fresh mental and spiritual attitude.)"

Slightly Bruised and a Little Broken

A MEMOIR

Petite Breaux

All rights reserved. No part of this book may be reproduced or transmitted in any form or by any means, graphic, electronic, or mechanical, including photocopying, recording, taping, or by any information storage retrieval system, without the permission, in writing from the copyright owner.
This is a work of fiction. Names, characters, places and incidents either are the product of the author's imagination to are used fictitiously, and any resemblance to any actual persons, living or dead, events or locales is entirely coincidental.

Copyright © 2015 by Petite Breaux
Revised edition October 2015

Edited by SAT

ISBN – 13: 978-0692541753
ISBN-10: 0692541756

To order additional copies of this book, visit:
www.amazon.com
www.petitebreaux.com

Acknowledgement

To My Family, I love you all.

Special thank you to my eldest daughter for remembering dates, times and events of the past.
Thank you to all of my children for loving me through all of the difficulties. Thank you to my mother for loving me unconditionally.
Thanks to my significant other for always being there.

I thank God for giving me strength and courage to move forward.

Contents

Introduction
One ~ Fatherless Daughter...................1
Two ~ Molested...................7
Three ~ Truancy...................11
Four ~ Fifteen and Pregnant...................14
Five ~ Teenage Abuse...................17
Six ~ Family Drama................... 21
Seve   Teenage Marriage...................28
Eight ~ Just Try It...................32
Nine ~ Taking One for the Team................... 35
Ten ~ Something To Do................... 38
Eleven ~ Shatter Dreams Meets A Cry For Help...41
Twelve ~ Who Said The Grass Was Greener 82
Thirteen ~ Why Pay For The Cow? 87
Fourtee ~ Could This Be My Soul Mate?...............93
Fiftee ~ Wrongful-Termination...................106
Sixtee ~ Where Is The Love? 116
Conclusion................... 124

Introduction

This book was written to help others, not that my story is anything new in life, but maybe the way I tell it will allow someone to relate and feel less alone. My thought was that keeping things quiet about my life was best and it wouldn't affect me in the long run. I was wrong, I had a voice and I should have used it, told someone what was happening with me and to me.

I used to be that person that used to ask the question, why would anyone stay in violent types of relationships? Not anymore, because if you have not been in that person's shoes, you just cannot imagine the reasoning for some of the things we do or don't do.

I have learned that looking from the outside in can be very misleading. My past has affected me in certain aspects of my life that I have never given thought too.

Our past life doesn't define the person we are today. We all have gone through something in our lives.

Whether it's chaos, drama, failed relationships, dysfunctional family or employment we have experienced those less than happy moments in life. By sharing my past experiences, I am trying my best to cope with life, not letting anything hold me back.

People always comment that I don't smile, well what I say to that is, it doesn't mean I'm not happy. My life is not perfect. Do I wish it could be better? Yes! I have so many parts of life I think about, I often find my thoughts are all over the place, as was my life since childhood. As children, we sometimes mock our parents' lifestyles. Although my children know I love them, it was never verbally or physically shown as it should have been. I regret this. I have plenty regrets I cannot take back; all I can do is try not to make those same mistakes.

I am still trying to be a better mother, a better daughter, a better person. I was a young mother of three by the age of twenty-two. I had to become a mature, responsible person early in life. No one to blame but myself. I didn't have the chance to enjoy my adolescent years like others my age.

My mother did so much for my children and me. I could never repay her. Even as a child, I would always tell her I would move out the second I turned eighteen. I would leave home and live on my own. I was a hardheaded child, and I did not like to listen. I wanted to do things my own way. But I kept my word. I left home at eighteen and went back to The Parrish to live with my grandmother for a while.

I tried to raise my children with a little more freedom than I actually had. I wanted them to experience life and know what it meant to be responsible. They never got what they wanted—nor needed—all the time, but it made them more appreciative. I did what I had to do to make it. I never received a penny of child support from either of my children's father, and I never kept their children away from them. I made the kids go with them even when they did not want to go.

This was my time, and it let them get to know their father, so they could make their own decision on how they felt about him. I never told my children anything negative about their fathers; it was not my place. Every child should know his or her parents and their siblings.

My life would be complete if I could only see and spend time with my grandchildren. For now, I just have to say okay to this situation and let go.

I used to feel that I had to get revenge on all those who had wronged me. How, I didn't know. Some I would just curse out, and for others, I would just keep the hatred for them inside of me. Despite this, I love helping others. I would give my last to help another, but I don't like to be taken advantage of or used. A male friend of mine told me that as long as I continued to be as nice as I was, then I would always leave myself open to—be—"fucked"—over.

Any form of abuse is not acceptable. Abuse does not look good nor does it feel good. Stop the abuse, the rape, domestic violence, and molestation. Keeping Silent is not the answer.

~One~
FATHERLESS DAUGHTER

My mother raised me as she saw fit. It was her way of protecting me from society. She did an excellent job; I had all the material items a young girl could want. I dressed well; my hair was always combed into pigtails with ribbons and bows. With all of that, I knew my mother loved me, but the physical love was missing. I thought maybe this was because it was absent in her childhood.

It was just her and I for a long period.

My mother, Francine, was a very strict woman. Dishes had to be washed a certain way, beds had to be made a certain way, clothes had to be folded a certain way, and the house had to be cleaned a certain way. Everything had to be done a certain way. If none of this were done correctly, I would have to redo it all over again.

She did not believe in me hanging out with friends or going to school dances. I loved getting out of the house. I was always somewhere I should not be, and once Francine found out, I got a whipping. I was always getting a whipping, not only for being elsewhere, but also for my smart mouth and for my lying to get out of trouble. It only got worse as I reached my teenage years.

As a teenager, I was not happy with certain looks about myself; I thought that my nose and my ears were too big.

I did not have many friends. I felt this was because I was different, a loner, not part of the in crowd.

I took band in school and played the flute. I went out for track and made the team. It was a bit of freedom, but as fast as I made the team, I lost my position for being smart with my teacher. I had to find freedom elsewhere. That's when I took advantage of the times I could spend nights at my aunt's house with my cousins, and I stayed with my grandmother as much as possible—I had freedom again.

Because I did not have the freedom I would have liked to have, I was skipping school and snuck around.

I used to love being outdoors all day, riding my bike, skating on the sidewalk, playing hopscotch, jumping rope, playing marbles and hide-and-seek, and going to the park to use the merry-go-round and the swings.

Sometimes, I would see fathers playing with their daughters at the park and be reminded of my own situation. I knew of my father, but I wasn't raised with him in the home or in my life. My mother and father were not married when I was born, and a few months after my birth, my father had another girl pregnant, so he chose not to be there for my mother and me. A year later, my father married and had a new baby girl.

I'm not sure how long he was married the first time, but sometime later, my father remarried a second time and had two sons.

I have always known about my younger sister and brothers. I remember meeting my sister and actually playing with her as a child; her mother and my mother even became friends.

My father never established a relationship between my younger siblings, but after all, why would he when he never established a relationship between he and I? These family dynamics caused some rather unusual moments.

One time, when I was in the sixth grade, I was riding the city transit—as many kids did back then for transportation to and from school—and I was on my way to Saint Thomas Catholic School in The Parrish.

That day, while riding the bus home, I saw this little boy about four years my junior. He looked so familiar to me, and then, it dawned on me. He was my younger brother. He was getting off at his stop, so I decided to do the same. I never said anything to him, but I continued to follow him and he just kept looking back at me. I wanted to get to know him, but after a few blocks, I just turned around and headed back in the direction of my home.

That next Saturday, I searched the Yellow Pages to find my dad's phone number. When I found it, I called the number and a small boy answered.

"Can I speak to Joseph?" I asked.

"This is Joseph."

"No. Your father Joseph."

"Who is this?"

"Your sister Simone".

"You're not my sister!" he shouted. "I only have one sister, Margarite." Then, he hung up the phone.

I never called again.

I tried on several occasions to establish a relationship with my father. As a small child around the age of ten or eleven, I would cross the wide and busy streets of The Parrish all by myself. I would walk to my father's home and knock on his front door. Never invited in, he would come out onto the porch.

He always came across as very uncomfortable because he was looking back at his front door, as if he didn't want his wife to know that I was there on her front porch. In a matter of minutes, I would be leaving. He showed no interest. He never once questioned this small child, his daughter, walking those streets alone. Did you walk over here by yourself? Does your mother or anyone know where you are? Nothing at all.

I would then walk up the street to his father's house where I was welcomed. One day at my grandfather's home, I first saw my youngest brother.

He was only about eleven months old; there wasn't any way he would remember me.

When I was thirty-two, my children and I, for the first time ever, were invited to my father's home. This was when I first actually met my two younger siblings. I didn't know what to expect, but I was not impressed. My thoughts were, as always, you could not miss what you never had. I believe now that this is not true for everyone.

Now that my father is sick, we are trying to reunite and establish a father-daughter relationship, for me at the age of fifty-one; I didn't care either way, but was open to talking with him.

I recently visited my father. He and his two sons were having a conversation about events they shared in the past.

One son was on the telephone and the other was visiting, as was I. I just sat there and listened, and I could not relate or join in on their reminiscing. This disturbed me, and I didn't know why. Even then, my youngest brother and I are trying to establish a relationship.

It is hard because I wasn't raised with his father, so I do not know his father as he does. I cannot share that conversation with him. He would say, "Our father," and I would say, "Your father."

When I speak of this young man, I only mention his name when in conversation, and then, I am asked, "Who is this person?" I just tell them he's my father's son. In response, I get, "Your brother?" I just say yes.

Slightly Bruised and A Little Broken

    Now my children know their fathers, but they weren't raised with either of them in the home or as a part of their lives. I can sometimes see that growing up without a father has affected my youngest daughter. I know as a mother that my son needed a father figure in his life growing up.

    Although I did all that I could, it wasn't enough. Sometimes I wonder if not having a father in my life has bruised me in some ways when it comes to relationships.

~ Two ~
MOLESTED

Mother paid close attention and noticed everything that went on with me as a child. However, my mother was unaware that her stepdad, Liam, was molesting her ten-year-old child. I was living out of town with my grandparents. My mother was not there.

I don't blame her for not being aware; she thought I would be safe with my grandparents.

My grandfather Liam was a solid man, six feet two inches tall and somewhere around a solid two hundred and fifty pounds. I was a small child weighing about sixty pounds. I remember the pain and the discomfort. It made me sick to my stomach. No one ever questioned it.

Several years ago, I wrote it all in a letter to my mother, Francine. She became angry and said my grandfather had better be glad he was already dead, because if were not, she would surely kill him now. I am sure she felt guilty, because from my birth, her focus was to keep me close, fed, well dressed, and protected.

I lived with my grandparents during the years from time to time to attend school and for summer vacation. Liam was the only grandfather I ever knew, and I loved being around him. He gave me everything I wanted. We went to the dog shelter where he bought me a puppy.

I named him Rex.

Liam and I went fishing often. He would get me into the back of the camper. There, he would undress me and have his way.

When I stayed home from school, my grandmother would leave me home with Liam. That is often when he would take advantage of me. I was so used to this happening that I expected it. When it did not happen, I went to Liam for attention, and he pushed me away.

I can recall a time when I stayed home from school not feeling well. I had a fever, so I was sleeping curled up on two chairs in my grandmother's bedroom. Liam came over, pulled my pants down, pulled me by my legs closer to him, and penetrated me. I have kept this to myself for over forty-five years—kept my mouth shut. I don't know why I stayed silent so long, but I sure wish I had told someone then. Liam told me not to tell anyone about what we did. This continued on through sixth grade.

One day, it just stopped; my grandfather did not touch me again. The only explanation

I can recall is because he and my grandmother moved back to Oleander City to be around my mother and other family members. Whatever the reason, I am glad it stopped.

Who gave this man permission to take my virginity, to abuse me so? This has haunted me throughout my life, distorting my relationships and interactions with men, and holding me back from finding love.

Was this, what Liam showed me, how to love someone?

Slightly Bruised and A Little Broken

~ Three ~
TRUANCY

When I was fourteen, my mother married Nathan. We were living in Oleander City. Nathan, my mother's husband, purchased a new home on the other side of town. After we moved, I met several new friends and neighbors. I met Leonard, who was seventeen, three years older than I was. Francine, my mother, was not having this. She said Leonard was too old for me and that I could not see him. Nevertheless, Leonard and I continued seeing each other. I snuck around and skipped school to hang out with him.

One particular day, I skipped school with Leonard and his cousins, and I got terribly drunk from drinking dark Bacardi rum straight. I was running around the car. The boys chased me to get me back in the car, and the rest of the day is a blur for me. I remember being at his house. I remember walking up the street to my house, still somewhat drunk. Leonard and his cousins were too scared to bring me home, so they dropped me off on the corner. I was not in the best condition.

Francine was waiting for me at home, standing in the front door. She called the police. I just wanted to lie down and go to sleep. Francine gave me a beating that was out of this world. My body was numb, so I felt no pain. She filled me with coffee, but it all came up. When the police officer got to the house and came inside, Francine told him she wanted to put me in juvenile detention. The police officer told her I had done nothing so bad that would require me to go to juvenile detention. Francine was still mad as the officer told her the only charge against me would be truancy. This was my first offense that he knew of, so he let it go.

Francine called her sister to ride with her to the hospital. She was determined to have me examined. She had convinced herself I had been raped. That did not happen.

The boys told me I was left outside in a chair because they did not want me throwing up in their mother's house. They left me outside in the freezing winter cold. Heck, I don't remember. Skipping school and being truant was fun, but it was causing problems for Francine and Nathan.

Petite Breaux

~ *Four* ~
FIFTEEN AND PREGNANT

Gabe lived just up the hill from me. I could see his house from our bathroom window. I had not met him earlier because he was out of town for the summer. We went to the same school, and I did not like him. I thought he was strange. His cousin called me one day asking if I could give him a chance. I fell for it and said okay. We started talking on the phone, and I went up to his house.

Each morning we would walk to the school bus stop together.

We started dating. I started skipping school again to be with him. I got pregnant, and my mother beat me with a hairbrush. My mother told me I was not keeping the baby. My actions had hurt her. I did not want an abortion; I wanted to keep the baby.

Nevertheless, my mother insisted, so it was done. I was sad and angry because my opinion did not matter.

The doctor asked what I wanted to do, but he told me that since I was only fifteen, it was not my decision. My mother made me get the abortion. The aborted baby was a boy. I was in so much pain from the abortion.

When I arrived home, I just went in my room, headed straight for my bed, and fell asleep. Later that night, the pain woke me up, and I started to cry as my thoughts ran wild about what had happened. I was mad at my mother.

Not being able to do what I wanted to do upset me so much that I just wanted to die. I went into the bathroom with razor in hand to end my life. I held my wrist out and tried to slice it with the sharp razor. *Owwww!* It hurt like hell. I didn't like the pain, but I tried another slice. *Owwww! Owwww!* I was jumping up and down. *Nope, forget it.* I ran my wrist under some cold water, wiped off the blood, and thought to myself, *How does anyone do this?* My cuts were not deep at all, but enough to leave marks that looked like scratches. I never gave it another thought.

Another six months or so went by, and I became pregnant again. I did not know it at the time, so when mother asked if I were pregnant, I said no, but she said, "Yes, you are, doing all that spitting." She knew before I did. I was a sophomore in high school and pregnant for the second time.

That September, I had a beautiful baby girl, Sharmayne. I now had my own baby, someone to call my own, someone to love and someone to love me. I was good at taking care of Sharmayne. I kept her fed, clean, and smelling good.

I would go to school, and my mother would take Sharmayne to the babysitter's on her way to work.

Nathan was good with Sharmayne. He loved her, and she was his pumpkin. He would always fall asleep in the rocking chair with Sharmayne on his shoulder.

Any time school was out, Sharmayne was all mine. Sharmayne was my responsibility. I made sure she always had clean bottles and baby formula prepared each day. I had her bottle and bottle warmer in my room, so that I would be ready for her night feedings.

~ *Five* ~
TEENAGE ABUSE

I was still dating Gabe, but he was changing and not for the better. He was not good for me at all. He was controlling.

One day at his house, we were down in the basement. I did not want to sleep with him, and he put a belt around my neck and pulled it so tight I could not breathe. I struggled to break free. I was gagging. The belt was getting tighter. My eyes felt as if they were going to pop out of my head.

The doorbell rang, and this saved me. I do not want to imagine how this could have ended up. He went upstairs to answer the door. It was his uncle. I took that opportunity to leave and go home. I ran up the street to my house.

I was afraid. I looked in the mirror, and my face was extremely red. I had broken out with little red bumps.

I continued dating Gabe all through high school. I was pregnant again my senior year. "Every day I had morning sickness, I had to excuse myself from class." I would never make it to the restroom, so I just threw up in the hallway. I was missing so many days at school that I was not going to have enough credits to graduate.

When the end of the school year approached, I was eight and a half months pregnant. I was not going to walk with my class. I registered to take my GED test. When asked when the baby was due, I said two weeks, and they made an exception to let me take the test the next day. I passed. Cecilia was born about a week later. I was determined to have that diploma the year I was to graduate. I stopped dealing with Gabe when Cecilia was about two months old.

I had a new boyfriend. At this time, we had moved from the house with Nathan into a townhouse down on Wyoming Court. Mother and Nathan were divorcing. My mother and her sisters had gone out of town for the weekend, so I invited a few friends over. We played cards, laughed, talked, and drank. Later that night, everyone had fallen asleep.

Early the next morning, I heard someone knocking at the door, so I quietly went downstairs. I did not want to wake anyone. I opened the door to Gabe. I thought to myself, *What is he doing here so early in the morning?*

That's when he pushed me aside and came in. I told him to leave, to not make a scene, that the girls were asleep. I didn't want to wake anyone else in the home, as it would have ended badly. Gabe went upstairs. I pulled him by his shirt, and he turned and hit me right behind my ear with the butt of his gun. I was bleeding and a little dazed. Still, no one heard a thing.

Gabe pulled me out the front door, saying he was going to kill me. He pushed me into the car and pulled me by my hair. Early in the morning, no one outside. The streets were empty. No one heard the struggle. I should have screamed. I just balled my eyes out.

He drove to an empty area and kept threatening to kill me. We struggled in the front seat of the car. He overpowered me, ripped my pants off, and had his way, and then he took me back home. I then woke everyone in the house, and we went to the hospital.

I told Gabe's uncle what had happened, and he went looking for him. I told the police what had happened. I filed charges, but they could not find him.

I left the hospital with stitches and went home. Gabe was nowhere to be found. When my mother returned home, I did not utter a word. I made up a story about how I hit my head on the sharp edge of the sconce that was hanging on the wall in the stairway.

Slightly Bruised and A Little Broken

~ Six ~
FAMILY DRAMA

Nathan and my mother's marriage was going good, except for those times when Nathan had been drinking. Eventually, those episodes got out of hand. He would come home and pick fights with my mother. At times, I would hear them arguing and him threatening my mother. One time, I ran downstairs, screaming at him, shouting at him not to hit my mother. He came over to where I stood on the stairs, and he backhanded me something fierce. He told me to go back to my room. I ran back upstairs to my room, crying and afraid. I locked my bedroom door, checked on Sharmayne, and stayed awake all night.

The next day, I left and went to stay with my aunt. I had no intentions of going back to that house. Sometimes I believed that I was the problem in their marriage. He would always break the frames that held my picture. I would always hear my name in their arguments.

When Nathan came to my aunt's home to speak with me about that night, he apologized and said it was never going to happen again. He even asked me to come back home. I decided to return home, not because he asked me to, but because of my mother.

After a couple of the drinking mishaps with Nathan, things were not the same. I was afraid each night Nathan came home from work. If he slammed the door behind him,

I knew he was drunk and an argument would happen. My mother decided she would leave him. While outside loading our belongings in the car, an argument started.

"You are not taking this car," Nathan said to my mother.

Nathan had bought this car for her, and we were not leaving in it. She was taking her car.

"I don't see what difference it makes," my mother said.

"We'll see about that!"

Nathan went inside through the garage door to our basement. I was still standing outside. My mother went inside to call her sister and her mother. I didn't know if this was the right move to make. I should have called the police first to let them establish some order and make the situation as peaceful as possible.

But that is not how it happened.

Petite Breaux

My aunt, my cousin, my grandmother, and my uncle all showed up at the same time. Everyone was outside arguing. The neighbors were in their doors.

The look in Nathan's eyes that day was as if he were another person. He went back inside, and I went behind him. He was coming with the rifle, and I hid behind the rocking chair in the living room. He didn't see me.

I went inside to get my baby Sharmayne. She was asleep in her swing. My grandmother was outside standing on the other side of the street. She decided to use the neighbor's phone to call Liam.

She told Liam, "You need to get over to Francine's house—now."

"I'm not coming over there," Liam said. "You need to come home and stay out of it."

Liam was just home from a day of fishing. My grandmother insisted that Liam come and to bring his gun.

My uncle argued with Nathan out on the street. Liam arrived, speeding up the road. He parked the truck on the other side of our drive by the shrubbery. Liam got out and moved to the center of the street.

My uncle moved to the other side of Nathan's truck. Looking at Nathan, he said something with a smile on his face, like a smirk. Nathan fired a shot at him but missed. The bullet blew out the window of my grandfather's truck. My uncle ducked down behind the truck. It was downright terrifying.

While Nathan was at the end of the sidewalk, I grabbed Sharmayne and ran down the hill to my grandmother's car, where my cousin and aunt were sitting inside. I tossed Sharmayne onto the back seat and ran back into the house.

I did not want to leave my mother. My aunt and cousin were so afraid, they had put the car in the wrong gear and were pressing the gas pedal—*brrrrmmmm*—just burning rubber and not going anywhere.

My cousin finally got the car in drive and sped off.

In the meantime, back in the house, I got to the phone and called the police.

My mother, Francine, was out in the street trying to keep hidden behind parked and moving cars to avoid a bullet. Nathan kept pointing that rifle in her direction as if he were on a duck hunt. He was definitely trying to kill her.

Meanwhile, my grandfather was in the middle of the street fiddling with his ancient itty-bitty gun, trying to fire at Nathan. What a mistake that was. Nathan pointed that rifle and pulled the trigger. The bullet lifted my grandfather off his feet. Hit in the groin, down to the ground, he fell hard.

I stood in the screen door, watching the whole thing. I screamed so loud—screaming, screaming! I was shaking, crying frantically. Nathan turned when he heard my scream, his eyes still crazy as if he were possessed. Nathan headed in my direction toward the house. I dropped to my knees, crawled quickly, and hid behind the rocker. I heard the door open. I kept as quiet as I could. I was so scared of what he might do if he saw me. Nathan went to the kitchen, but he came back into the living room where he saw me hiding. He pointed the gun at me and said, "Get," and I got!

I ran out the front door and down the hill in the front yard over to where Liam lay in the street. I grabbed Liam's gun and ran inside the neighbor's home.

I saw Nathan come back outside, pointing that rifle at whoever was out there. He looked like a lunatic, eyes red and face stern.

I asked my neighbor to check the gun to make sure it was loaded. I wanted to shoot Nathan dead, I was so angry with him.

My neighbor told me to wait for the police, and he held onto the gun. I waited impatiently for the police to arrive. I heard the sirens. They were getting closer.

Finally, they arrived, the ambulance following suit.

About four police officers jumped out of their vehicle, weapons drawn on Nathan. One officer shouted to Nathan, "Drop the weapon!" Nathan did not respond. The officer repeated himself a second time, "Sir, drop the weapon." Nathan did not turn around and kept his back to the officers. Nathan hesitated, but he laid the rifle down and raised both hands. The officers rushed toward Nathan, bombarded him to the ground, and handcuffed him.

Liam was in the ambulance; they were working on him. I overheard them say that they had to remove the left testicle. The pellets from the shotgun had penetrated Liam's body throughout. He was bleeding badly, and the paramedics were trying to save his life.

Once at the hospital, they said he was a fighter, strong as a horse, and thought he would pull through.

But Liam died the next day.

This was a tragedy.

I was sixteen and could not take it. My knees just went weak. I fell right where I stood. The news hit everyone hard. It was extremely hard on Francine, since Liam was her stepfather and Nathan was her husband.

My grandmother arranged to have Liam's body taken back to The Parrish where he would be buried. After Liam's burial, we returned home.

The time had come to determine Nathan's sentence for the murder of Liam.

We went to court, and they heard testimony from everyone who was involved. Nathan was cleared on self-defense, and I believe the decision was based on my testimony. I told the truth as I saw it.

With the family there, things escalated, and Nathan felt ganged up on.

If the family had stayed home and not interfered, Liam would have lived. This was my belief. If my grandmother had listened to Liam and went home as he had asked, if she had not insisted that he come to our house, Nathan would not have shot him. "If this, if that", I thought. Someone would have been hurt that day, but no one would have died. I did not blame my grandmother for what happened to Liam. I knew she was just trying to protect her daughter from any hurt or harm.

We all do things in the heat of the moment to protect our own. Our sound judgment goes out the window and emotional reflexes kick in. My grandmother was torn by losing Liam this way. My mother was caught in the middle of her husband and her family. And our lives were never the same.

~ Seven ~
TEENAGE MARRIAGE

Sitting on my grandmother's screened-in front porch one evening, I watched the neighbors across the way have a party, with loud talking, loud laughter, and loud music. The song *"Supersonic"* was playing and I saw this boy dancing to it. He caught my eye. I was thinking I must meet him.

Who was he? Where did he live? *Who were his friends?*

I was resourceful, and I could find out later. You know, looking at someone far off can fool you, so I wasn't sure what I was seeing.

The next day, I inquired about this young man and found out that he lived around the corner, about two blocks away. Hmm, why had I never seen this boy? Anyhow, I met him. His name was Wardell, and we started dating. He was living with his mother, and

I was still at my grandmother's. I just wanted to be out on my own.

Wardell was a young boy, and he was always smiling. Wardell loved animals. He had pigeons, fifty-gallon fish tanks, piranhas, a pit bull, and a Great Dane. Yes, he had some animals. Wardell and I dated for a few months, and then I told him we should get married. He said okay.

I was the dominant one, and he was easygoing. We looked for a place and found one right across the street from his grandparents. We told his mother, and she asked if we would take her home while she moved into the place we found. She wanted to be close to her parents and her sister. We agreed because this would keep me close to my family and both our friends.

We went to the city hall to get our marriage papers. My mother purchased my dress, and she surprised us with a wedding cake. We invited a few friends and family over to my great-grandmother's home where we were married in her living room.

Wardell and I enjoyed each other's company. We did not argue or fight. We were young, nineteen and twenty, and this was like setting up house. Wardell had a regular job and I was working at the beauty salon. My girlfriends, Joyce and Teresa, and I all worked at the salon together. We would meet up in the mornings on the city transit.

Wardell and I moved into our new place, and I started to notice Wardell's habits that I had not been aware of previously. There was nothing big, but some were bothersome. *What did I expect from Wardell?* He had been living at home with his mother, with no responsibilities, and here comes this young girl with two small children, ages one and three. *Did I expect him to become an instant dad or even know how to be a father?* My expectations were high, and it was not fair.

Wardell was a constant soda drinker. He could not be active out in the sun for too long or he would suffer a heat stroke. I thought if this continued, Wardell would turn into a hospital bill.

One day, before heading out to church, I left a roast in the oven on a slow cook. When I came home, Wardell had eaten the roast. I was heated and so angry with him. I was getting tired of his habits and soda drinking, which wasn't good for his health. Sometimes, it would cause skin discoloration.

Then, Wardell came home one day with a big python snake. I was furious. He put that snake in the aquarium the kids and I had to pass every day to get to the front door. The lid was not secure. That snake could get out and strangle my girls or even me. I was not having it. I told Wardell, "Either you get rid of the snake, or we are leaving."

Our marriage could have lasted longer than a year, but for me, it was over. I asked for a divorce. Wardell did not want it, but we separated, and I went back to live with my mother, grandmother, and great-grandmother.

Whenever I would contact Wardell about going to the courthouse to sign the papers, he kept biding time, saying he was too busy to go.

One day I said, "No more excuses." I picked him up, and we drove to the courthouse to finalize our divorce.

It was not a bad breakup. We were two very young kids who did not know what we were doing at the time.

I have not spoken with Wardell in years, but I do keep in touch with his mother—great in-laws, great family, very loving.

Moving fast and wanting to get out and be on my own, I put Wardell and myself in a situation for which neither of us was ready.

~ Eight ~
JUST TRY IT

When I was nineteen, I moved back to The Parrish where I met Luther. He drove a little red Corvette. He was much older than I was. We went out to eat, and then, we got a room for a few hours at the hotel. He had a little foil package in his possession, and he opened it, gesturing for me to try it. I refused. I didn't want to do that. "Well, just rub a little on your teeth," he repeatedly said.

I gave in to his request, and I did just a little bit. It was white powder cocaine, and I was afraid of what it might do to me.

I would say I was a gullible girl growing up. I believed almost everything Luther said to me or anyone else for that matter. I was looking for something in my life. Something had been missing, and I was looking in all the wrong places and faces for that lost soul.

Later, Luther drove me home, and that was the end of us. I saw him around the neighborhood from time to time, with nothing but a hello, how you doing, and a good-bye.

Cocaine was a drug that I was not interested in trying ever again. Thank goodness that my willpower was stronger than that desire.

Slightly Bruised and A Little Broken

~ Nine ~
TAKING ONE FOR THE TEAM

I was downtown in The Parrish at one of the Boardwalk hotels. I was maybe twenty years of age. My girlfriend Joyce called to invite me out. Joyce said she had met a man and wanted me to meet his friend. You know, taking one for the team. I agreed to meet them. She told me to meet her at the hotel where they were staying.

My memory of this night is somewhat unclear. I do remember wearing my favorite dark orange corduroy pants. I cannot remember how I ended up in the hotel room with some man Joyce had just met or how I ended up getting caught up in that mess. For the life of me, I do not remember this man's name at all. I do remember him having a perm and that he played professional ball, but I don't know if that was true or not.

Slightly Bruised and A Little Broken

He was a very large man, wide in stature, and tall. I did not know where Joyce had disappeared, but I was getting uncomfortable, being left alone in a room with a man who was supposed to be her date. I was preparing to leave when he grabbed my arm and threw me on the bed. I begin to yell and scream in hopes that someone in the hotel would hear my cries. He smothered my mouth with his huge hand and held it there. He was much too heavy for my small body frame to escape his capture. I pleaded with him not to hurt me. I just wanted to go home to my daughters. I cried and cried, and thought to myself, *Why did Joyce leave me here alone?*

He continued to control my body and did not stop until he was finished doing his business. I got up frightened, glazed with shock, and I did not speak a word. I grabbed my purse, abruptly left the room, and headed home.

Once I arrived home, I tiptoed into the house. Still in shock, I was quiet as a mouse, because I did not want to wake my daughters or my mother. I took a bath and never mentioned the rape to anyone. I know this sounds insane; it was so very long ago. I never talked about it and kept it dormant in my mind until now.

As I sit and reminisce over my younger years, I realize the psychological factors that have played into my adulthood life. That night, I realized, was rape, and for the first time, despite the other times, I faced that fact, and I felt like I had become a statistic.

When I talked to Joyce that next morning, she said that she was tipsy and had the other man take her home. I knew she had too much to drink, but I did not know she was leaving me alone. I did not tell her what had happened, but maybe I should have. I did not want her to feel guilty. Later, I found out the very next night Joyce was with this same guy that had just abused me the night before; she even spent the night with him. Joyce thought he was an okay person. I really should have opened my mouth to tell her, but I don't think she would have believed me.

Our friendship faded. She was on one side of town and I was on the other, and I told myself that was why, but perhaps, that was just the excuse I told myself.

The events of that night could have affected our friendship and me more than I knew.

~ Ten ~
SOMETHING TO DO

I was working downtown at one of the hotels as a housekeeper. My baby girls were still going to daycare while I worked. I met William. He always hung out across the street with my neighbors. They introduced us to one another. He was a truck driver. He came over to the house for me to cut his hair. From that day on, we started a romance. I became intimately involved with him. I wasn't into William really, just something to do, but I became pregnant with Melik. William and I discussed the pregnancy. William asked me not to give the baby his last name. I listened. When I was about two months pregnant, I decided I wanted to move back to Oleander City.

I packed up the girls, and we took the Amtrak train home. In Oleander City, my children and I stayed with my cousin. While there, I applied for government assistance.

When Melik was born, I did not keep my word to William. I did not name Melik a junior, but he did get William's last name. William was not a great father; he did not even try to be a father to Melik. He was full of lies and deception. He would call sometimes and talk about what he was sending Melik, just giving my son and I false hope.

We shouldn't have dared to wait on William's false intentions, because nothing ever came and he never called. I just stopped listening to William and allowing him to hurt my son in the process. I did not want my son to be disappointed repeatedly.

I never put demands on William. He has always been welcome to spend quality time with Melik. However, he made his choice and ignored his options. I chose not to communicate with William, but if he contacted us, I would speak with him, and I would allow Melik to talk to him.

Melik is all grown up and a father himself, and William is still William. He has tried on several occasions to reach out to Melik, but it is difficult. William has disappointed Melik too many times.

Slightly Bruised and A Little Broken

~ *Eleven* ~
SHATTERED DREAMS MEETS A CRY FOR HELP

I had known Christian since high school, where we attended the same school. We went out on one date but had interference from my ex-boyfriend at the time, Gabe, so we never tried it again.

Years later, I found out that my cousin, whom I was living with for a while, was dating Christian's brother. I told my cousin to send a message through his brother, telling him that I said hello.

At this time, I was pregnant with my son, Melik, but Christian and I had started having phone conversations, and then he started visiting me.

He was there for me during my pregnancy. I gave birth to Melik and gave him his father's last name, even though Christian and I were together. Christian was still hanging in there with the children and me.

Christian was about five-eight, with a stocky athletic build, and around one hundred sixty pounds.

Slightly Bruised and A Little Broken

He emphasized to me that he would never act like any other man, mistreating and hitting a woman, and I believed him.

I moved from my cousin's into a place of my own, and I started receiving government assistance.

Christian was in college, about forty-five minutes up the road. He would come home from time to time and be with the kids and me.

It was snowing really badly one night, and I was to pick up Christian from the college. I had borrowed my grandmother's car. I drove down to get Christian with Melik in the car with me. Driving that road was nothing to me. I would just put on the radio and keep driving. One of my favorites was a popular song back then titled *"Computer Love."* There at Christian's college, Melik and I stayed in his dorm room until Christian finished working in the college cafeteria.

On the way back to Oleander City, we stopped at his brother's apartment. Once there, Christian was showing off, talking to his brother and just acting like a wild child. I felt somewhat very disrespected. I got Melik, got in the car, and left Christian right there with his brother.

Christian did not think I would leave him, but I showed him. He was running behind the car in the deep snow, yelling my name, trying to stop me. But I kept it rolling and went home. I was nice but no fool. I was kind of a wild child myself.

The next morning, Christian came to see me and apologized. Everything was good for the time being.

The next year, 1986, I moved into a townhouse, and things between Christian and me started to change.

One day, I was outside with some neighbors and had Melik in my arms. Christian drove up and asked me to come inside, so I asked my neighbor to hold Melik for me. I did not know what Christian's problem was, but once I got inside, he started shouting at me, and I shouted right back. Next thing you know, this anger escalated and he unexpectedly slapped me across my face and punched a hole in the wall. My lip was busted and bleeding like a purple grape. I was crying frantically. I was shocked; Christian had never done anything like this before. What was his problem?

The neighbors outside had heard everything. I went to get my baby and brought him back inside. My neighbor asked if I was all right, and I said yes.

This behavior of Christian's began to become frequent, and so did the abuse. I was stressing, scared, and losing my hair to the point where I was balding. I decided to cut my hair short.

My children knew that I was being physically abused as well as my neighbors. No one else knew of these incidents. I, again, kept my psychological emotions hidden.

Some months later, Christian decided to move to Saxton for employment. One of his friends from high school lived there and told him to come on down. After a couple of months there, Christian asked me to marry him. I went to visit him, and we were married at a Saxton courthouse in August of 1986.

This meant that my children and I would be relocating to Saxton. I had furniture still in The Parrish that I had purchased while married to Wardell. The kids and I packed up clothes only and moved with Christian to Saxton.

I thought we would have a new start, but Christian did not have a place for us to live. He was sharing an apartment with Galen and his wife, Carla, who had also moved from Oleander City to Saxton. They were all friends from past years. It was a two-bedroom apartment.

It was summertime, and the kids were not in school. I got a job through an employment agency.

After a few weeks, I went back to The Parrish, and my family helped me move my furniture to Saxton.

The first couple of months went fine, but then Christian got on one of his abusive trips. I was going to leave him. My children did not deserve this behavior around them. I thought about it, but where were we going to go? We had no one in the area.

One night, I took the kids, and we went to the laundry room of the apartment complex to spend the night. The laundry room was not going to work, so we walked. I carried Melik, and the girls carried the blankets.

We went up the road to this abandoned mall, laid down the blankets, and tried to get some sleep. I heard a car. It was Christian, driving around looking for us. He did not see us, as it was dark. Staying there did not last long. A big cockroach ran across the floor. That was enough for us, and the ground was hard to boot. We picked up the blankets and headed back to the apartment. We got into Christian's car, where I thought we would be all night.

Then, some bright lights flashed in the car windows. It was the police. They had seen some activity in the car and stopped to check it out. I explained what had happened between Christian and me. They had me and the kids get out of the car and head to the apartment. They talked with Christian, and he was being sweet as ever. The police left, and we went back inside. It was a quiet night, but I had become afraid of Christian. I grew tired of the living situation there. My kids did not have a room of their own, and they were sleeping on the living room floor. Melik slept in his playpen.

I sent the kids back to The Parrish with my mother until I could improve our living situation.

Carla and I were working together regularly with the employment agency. I did not know what had happened between her and her husband, but she and her son moved back to Oleander City.

Things became very complicated for me.

In the three years of living in Saxton, we had moved about seven times. I continued to find work. Christian was working, but he was not good at bringing the money home. Christian was MIA most of the time.

I got us another place to live in, a place called the Creekwood Apartments. The kids were back home, and I was working at Sprint as a data-entry clerk. I met a woman there who was moving back to her hometown in Germany. She was selling her car.

Ironically, it was a two-door hatchback Sprint. I needed a car. Christian was never home. I explained that I did not have money to buy the car from her. She asked me to give her two hundred dollars and just take over the payments, which I did.

The car had a manual transmission, and I did not know how to drive a stick shift, but I kept driving and practicing in school parking lots until I got it down. Before too long, I could get to and from work with no problem.

Weeks later, my aunt died (rest her soul), so we drove my car to Oleander City for the funeral. We each had a chance to spend time with family. Oleander City was an eight-hour drive from our home in Saxton. We stayed about three days, and then headed back. That trip was when I really learned how to drive a manual transmission.

Back home, we were back to the usual, with the kids back to school, and Christian and me both back to work. Christian was working, but he was always coming home early. As much as Christian worked, he never seemed to have any money. We were struggling as usual; bills were barley getting paid, and there was not enough food in the apartment.

I wanted to go home to The Parrish to visit.

I had talked to Francine, and she helped me out with gas money. I planned the trip and drove to The Parrish with Christian and the children.

Once in The Parrish, Melik's dad wanted to come get him and spend time with him. I said that would be okay, and I told Christian that William would be picking up Melik for the evening.

Christian reacted. "If you let that happen, I'm going to beat your ass on the ride back to Saxton," he said in a quiet tone.

I quickly told this to Francine. *"What is his problem?"* she asked. "He better be just talking."

I understood how Christian felt about Melik's father wanting interaction. Christian felt that since William was not doing anything for Melik, and that he, Christian, had a bond with Melik, he was the only father Melik needed. I said that no matter what William did or didn't do, Melik was his child, and I would never keep him away from him.

This was William's issue, not mine. I wanted Melik to know his other family. Therefore, I just blew Christian off and went about my way. William picked up Melik, and Christian stayed inside, heated and looking crazy.

The next day, we were to head back home in the evening. Well, about one hour into our return trip, I was driving, Christian was in the front passenger seat, and the kids were in the back. I had a head full of rollers, just driving, not worried about a thing.

WHAM! Right across the face, Christian hit me hard with his fist.

Startled, I quickly pulled the car off the road onto the shoulder in a neck-jerking motion. I threw the car in park and swung both legs from beneath the steering wheel to the side, and turned to face Christian.

I started kicking Christian as if I were riding a bicycle. I shouted, "Are you serious? Have you lost your damn mind? In my face, you're going to hit me while I am driving? What you just did was enough for me to crash into another car, jeopardizing my children's safety."

The window was down, and rollers were falling out of my hair and onto the roadway. "I'm getting off the next exit, and I'm calling the police on your ass!"

I jumped out of the car, went into the gas station, and asked the attendant to call the police for me, telling him that my husband had just punched me in the face while driving.

Christian was behind me but somewhat standoffish, just listening. I went back outside to the pay phone and made a collect call to Francine, my mother. I told Francine what had just happened. "What's wrong with his ass?" Francine was very upset. "He is not going to get away with this. He just could not wait to act stupid." Francine was ranting.

My Uncle Willie was with Francine at the time. Francine was telling him what was going on.

Uncle Willie asked where exactly we were and told me to stay there, that they were on their way and for me not to leave. He said, "If Christian wants to hit a female, let him fight a man." Christian was listening to everything.

He immediately called his mother to say that I had called my uncle, who was on his way with a gun. Christian never told his mother what he had done for all this to be going on. Christian was good at omitting the truth to his mother. He always made it look as if I were the one cheating and fighting him. Who was she to believe? She did not live with us, and she did not know what was going on daily in our household.

Christian's mother asked him to put me on the phone. When I said hello, Christian's mom started going off. "If anything happens to my son, I'm going to get you Simone, you hear me?"

The police finally arrived, and they were questioning me. I told them the details of what happened and how Christian had threatened me the night before about what he would do. The police officer examined my face and saw the swelling on the bridge of the nose and the redness.

"Does it feel broken?" he asked.

"No."

"Do you want to press charges?"

"No, I just want to take my children home. Can you tell Christian to sit in the backseat the rest of the ride home and to keep his hands to himself?"

The children were upset by all the drama. I assured them everything was okay. It was getting late, and I was getting tired and still had a ways to drive.

"You're going to have to drive the rest of the way home," I told Christian.

While driving, he reached into the backseat, put his hand on my leg, and said, "Sorry."

I didn't care now to hear anything from him. He had done this so often that sorry didn't count.

We did not wait for Francine and Uncle Willie to arrive because I knew the situation would have ended up bad.

I contacted Francine at the next stop to let her know the details and that I was okay, but I started wondering what was going on with Christian.

That's when I played private investigator.

He would say he was going one place and actually go to another place. One day, he said he was going out with his friends, so I—with my woman's intuition—took a walk around the apartment complex. I found Christian's car parked elsewhere in the apartments. I then went home, got the spare car key I had made without his knowledge, and moved the car back in front of our apartment.

Now, when Christian came to get his car, it would not be there. I heard Christian and his friends pull up. I cracked the bedroom window. I wanted to hear what his friend was telling him.

"Dang dog, she got yo ass," Zeike said.

Christian came inside where I confronted him. I wasn't one to keep quiet in the relationship. I would always let Christian know that I knew what he was up to and that I didn't like it. Christian would always hit me in the face, and the children would hear and see it all. I would always call the police, but they would always just take Christian outside and talk to him or have him leave for a couple of hours.

Of course, Christian would always come back with his nice attitude. It would be another busted lip or bruised face for me, and I would continue to go to work.

The next time I was looking for Christian, I saw his car parked in front of another apartment building. I did not know exactly where he was, so I decided, with Melik on my hip, to knock on all the doors in that building until I found Christian. I eventually did, and this girl answered the door. She was about twice my size.

"Is Christian here?" I asked.

She closed the door somewhat, and I overheard her say, "It's your wife."

Christian came to the door. I just went off on him. I was screaming and yelling at him. "Here I am, waiting at home for you, and here you are, sitting in some bitch's apartment." The girl, her name was Cassie, swung open the door, and said, "Wait a minute. Who you calling a bitch?"

Cassie told Christian to get his baby, and Christian did just that. He took Melik out of my arms, and Cassie and I started fighting, rolling all the way down the hill. When the fight ended, I took Melik from Christian. I told him he was not worth fighting over and that I would not fight over any man. I left and headed home. Cassie and I both had scratches on our faces, but nothing serious.

Yep, Christian had been cheating on me. Moreover, he had the nerve to be mad at me for catching him. I was observant and did not need to hear anything about his cheating from any outsider. I could find out on my own.

I would see Cassie from time to time driving through the apartment complex. We would just look at one another and keep moving.

One day, I was driving Christian's car and was almost to our apartment when the car stopped and would not start up again. Cassie was passing by, and she noticed that I was having a problem. "Is everything okay?" she asked. I told her what was going on without hesitation. She got out of her car and asked, "Where is Christian?"

"Who knows? I just need to get the car out of the road."

"You think the two of us could push it?"

"We can try." And we did.

I thanked her, and that was it.

We both realized it wasn't our fault what had happened because of Christian's dishonesty.

One of Christian's friends from Oleander City, who was still living near us, had his girlfriend from Oleander City move to Saxton, and we became friends. Megan was her name.

Megan and I would hang out. She was a hard worker, as was I, and she had a small daughter about Melik's age. Megan and I had fun times together. We would try smoking weed and drinking liquor for fun. We both had two no-good men in our lives.

One night, Megan was over visiting, and I was to drive her home later that night. While driving Megan home in Christian's car, we were pulled over by the police because of a broken taillight. I had left the kids home in bed asleep. I knew I would not be long, so there was no need in waking them.

But then, the police said that they were taking me into custody. "Why are you arresting me for a broken taillight?"

I explained I had small children at home who were alone, so the police followed me back to my apartment where I had to get the children out of bed and go down to the station with them. Christian was not home yet. Megan had to tell him what had happened so he could come get the kids from the police station and take them home.

If it were not for Megan helping me contact my mother and family to get money to get me out of jail, Christian would have left me there. Christian wasn't trying to get me out, because he was cheating on me with a girl back home. Every time I would contact him from the jail, he tried to act as if he was doing all he could do.

"How are the kids doing?" I would always ask.

"They're fine," was always his response.

I came to find he was not taking care of them at all, not feeding them properly or anything. I called Christian's mother for the money I needed to get out of jail. She wired the money to Christian.

However, he never used it to pay my bail. Instead, he spent it. I had my mother wire the money to Megan. Megan posted bail for me. Three days passed before I was released.

When I arrived back at the apartment, I noticed a card sitting on the counter from the girl Christian was cheating on me with. The card was out in the open, just as if he were single. I did not say anything at that time, but I went to the pay phone and called this girl collect. She accepted the call because she thought it was her "stinker," as she called him.

I said, "No, not stinka, but stinka's wife." Where that came from, I have no idea. We talked, and I got all the information I needed. I was told that Christian had told her that we were separated and that I had moved back home. I was heated. For one, Christian had left me in that cold ass jail with little black worms crawling on the floor, sleeping on a cold metal table. There were only four bunks in the cell, with eight other females already in there. These females weren't worried about getting released; they knew the daily stay amount would add up to their fine.

I confronted Christian, and we had another fight. I was screaming, telling Sharmayne to call the police. I had the broom, and I was hitting Christian with it while trying to defend myself. Christian punched me in the mouth. My lip was busted, and it started to swell up right away.

The police came once again, but they didn't take Christian. They told him to leave for several hours. I had Asian neighbors, who offered the kids and me dinner for the night.

Christian had his family back home thinking that I was the problem. He was feeding them lies by deception, and they had no reason not to believe him. They were not there, and no one ever asked me any questions.

As the old saying goes, "Blood is thicker than water." I don't believe this is always true. There are situations when water may be a little thicker than blood.

The next morning, one of Christian's friends came over after work. They were out on the porch. I cracked the window to hear what they were saying. I was always opening a window. Christian was going on, rambling about how unappreciative I was, how he was working his ass off to make things comfortable, and how he bought all this new furniture for me.

When I heard all this, I yelled out the window, "Oh, Christian, stop lying. You have not bought a damn thing in here. I am the one paying the bills, and all this shit is rented." I made him look stupid for a change.

Well, after a while, there was not enough money coming in to pay the bills. I had to let all the rental stuff go and took time to look for another apartment before any eviction notice came. I found another apartment at the Maples Apartments, and we moved.

I did everything for Christian: made sure his lunch was packed, ironed his clothes for the entire week, and cooked dinner. Christian didn't have to do anything, and this went on for months.

Christian got a job that was regular. I was working at this beauty shop as a shampoo girl. I had no transportation, so I would walk several miles or ride a bike to get there. Christian was driving the car.

The kids had their own room with their own bathroom. It was a nice place. Christian was still fighting me. I was tired of the abuse and my children not having anything.

One night, after Christian went to sleep, I decided to put his clothes in the bathtub, and I set them on fire. I wrote on the bathroom mirror, "I HATE YOU."

That night I damn near burned down our apartment.

Slightly Bruised and A Little Broken

    Christian was abusing me again, and this time, I was too angry. I went off to the extreme, and he called the police on me. He claimed I was crazy. This time, he was the one with the busted lip and bruises all over his chest. I did not know how I did it, but I did. I didn't even remember the incident.

    When the police arrived, Christian told them to look at him and then look at me, that he was the one with the bruises. The female officer had a smirk on her face, like *Good for her*. See, they had records of all the domestic calls and of my past bruises. They left and told us to have a good night. Christian wanted to press charges, but it didn't happen.

    Christian decided a few days later that he didn't want the marriage any longer. He moved out, left the kids and me, and went to live with a friend. He did not tell me anything about leaving. I had to hear it from him over the phone. He left no money and did not help on the rent for that month. Without his income, we were not going to make it. The kids suffered. We had no food in the apartment and no money. We were hungry for days until I decided to ask my neighbors for food for the children. I explained the situation, and my neighbors who lived next door to me were awesome.

    They fed my kids day and night, and the neighbor upstairs came to assist too. I couldn't hold on to the apartment. I asked my mother to come get the children until I could get on my feet.

    I got a job as a cashier at Alfred's Grocery Store and moved into another apartment called the Core, which was not too far from the old apartment. While moving their furniture into the new apartment, I left the kids' mattress outside while I took other items inside. When I came back outside, the mattress was gone. I was upset and found it funny all at the same time. I thought to myself that whoever took it, must have been watching me move in and was waiting to get something.

Evidently, they needed a mattress. Whoever took the mattress was going to be mad though, because that mattress was pissy as hell from all of Cecilia's piss-filled nights. That child knew she could wet a bed, but it was all they had, and I just kept trying to freshen it up. Now all the girls had to sleep on was a box spring. I covered it with extra blankets to cushion it somewhat. I thought by the time the girls came back from The Parrish that I would have had enough money to purchase them another mattress.

Eventually, we all settled in, and one night, I caught a ride home from a co-worker. I walked up the stairs to my apartment and opened the door, startled. Christian was sitting on the couch with one of my kitchen butcher knives in his hand. The first thought that ran through my mind was, *How did he get in?*

"What are you doing in my apartment? What do you want?" I was not afraid but concerned that he had a knife.

"I got in through the patio door," he said. This meant he had to climb up the balcony. "I was waiting to see if you were bringing anyone home, and if you had, I was going to kill you both."

"What are you doing in my apartment? What do you want?" I repeated to Christian in a stern voice. "You need to leave, or I am calling the police."

To my surprise, he left, but I did not trust him.

Once Christian was out the door and down the steps, I locked every window and door. Christian was still living with his friend Zeike, as he had since he left the kids and me in the Maples apartment. It was time for school to start, and the kids would be returning home.

At this time, I still had no car and was worried about how Cecilia would get to and from school. It was really too far for a four-year-old to walk. I had no choice but to put Cecilia alone, at four years of age, on the city transit bus, but I had talked to the bus driver. "If you could, please make sure that Cecilia gets off at her stop?" He understood and did not mind at all, but I was taking a chance with any stranger. Cecilia was in pre-K for half of a day, going in the afternoon, and she would walk home with Sharmayne. I worried constantly about having Cecilia ride the bus alone. Anything could have happened, and I knew I could not live with myself if anything happened to my baby. I could not ride with her. Finances were tight, and I had to make sure I kept enough change for Cecilia's bus ride. Cecilia was not happy with my decision. She was small and afraid, and I had her making big-girl decisions. This only went on for a short while.

I don't know how it happened or when, but Christian and I got back together. After a few months, I got us another, bigger apartment across the way from where we were. Therefore, we moved into the

Vines Apartments. Everything was good for a few months.

I took the test for the post office, and I was still working at Alfred's full time. I was offered a position within the post office, but it would not be permanent until I passed a twelve-hour course. I went in five times a week and spent the first hour coding by memorization and the rest of the night out on the dock sorting mail.

I was always worried about not being hired on because of my lack of transportation. Christian had his car, but he sometimes did not want me to make it to work. He would not take me there or pick me up. I started asking around at work if anyone lived near my area and would not mind carpooling. No one lived out my way; everyone lived in the opposite direction.

One person asked me exactly where I lived and that maybe he could help me out. He went on to ask how often I would need the ride. He could not pick me up every day, but he could try to help me out. His name was Diesel. He was a nice person. I had seen him around the docks, but I had never talked to him. So I had a ride. I was happy.

I would never let Diesel drop me off in front of my apartment but always around or at the corner.

I knew Christian was crazy and would not understand another man giving me a ride home. He was a jealous fella. I did not care who was giving me a ride home as long as I made it to work. All that mattered was keeping this job and getting it on a permanent basis. I knew this would be the key to me and the children starting a new life and being okay. I did not want anything to jeopardize this. We were struggling at home. I continued to get a ride to and from work with Diesel.

One evening, Diesel dropped me at the corner. He would usually park at the front of the apartment complex. I did not know that Christian had a friend living in that building, and one night, he saw Diesel drop me off. So, you guessed it, this person told Christian he saw me get out of this white Riviera with dark tinted windows. Christian did not say anything to me about this for a week or so. He was doing his own watch.

Christian was waiting one night for Diesel to drop me off, and we did not see him. When I turned the corner, I saw Christian take off on foot in the direction that Diesel's car was heading. I was scared out of my mind. I knew what was in store for me. I ran up the stairs to the apartment as fast as I could. I did not know what to do once I got inside. I just hid in the living room closet and prayed Christian would think I was not there. I knew this would only make matters worse.

I did not want to scare my children. They were in their beds asleep.

I always got home late when I worked the second shift.

Christian came back inside, slamming doors and yelling for me. I could hear him searching everywhere. When he did find me, he yanked me up by my hair and started punching and slapping me in the face. I was crying and pleading for him to stop. I usually tried to fight back to protect myself, but this would only make him more vicious. I was no match for Christian, even though he was not a big person. Once he stopped, he said, "Look at what you made me do."

And I, with my mouth, would respond, "I didn't make you do anything."

Christian said I always made him look like the villain, even though I was the one who ended up with busted lips and bruises. Christian always went for my face. I would just pick myself up, get myself together, and the next day, I'd head right back to work. If anyone questioned me about my face at work, I would answer with the truth. Diesel did not like this, but there wasn't much he could do. He had a family of his own. He felt sorry for me and wanted to help, but all he could do was keep my spirits up. Diesel continued to give me a ride home, even if he had to get someone from work to do it for him.

Life went on as usual for a few months. Christian would feel sorry and lay low for a while. He had always promised he would never hit me.

I was struggling daily to memorize my coding to past my test in the allowed time for the post office.

It had begun to snow. The weather was bad, and the kids needed something to eat in the apartment. I decided that the girls and I would catch the bus to the grocery store. They bundled up real good.

Christian stayed home with Melik.

At the store, I picked up a few things that we would be able to carry. We stayed inside the store until I saw the bus coming up the road. The plan was to run out in just enough time to catch the bus. Sharmayne and I were running, but I looked back and saw Cecilia was not making it. She could not catch up. Mind you, Cecilia was a lazy child, and nothing moved her. She was a little plump at that age of five.

So, we missed the bus. I was a little upset because I knew another bus would not be coming until an hour later or not at all. The weather was awful, with deep snow, ice, and cold winds. I knew that it was best we start walking home before things got worse.

This turned out to be the wrong decision.

With groceries in hand and two small children—five and seven years of age—this was the most horrible walk ever.

Cecilia was crying and just having a hard time. Our feet were frozen, our hands were cold, and home seemed forever away. We were sliding and slipping on the ice. Traction was awful and just not happening.

When we finally made it home, almost frostbitten to death, Christian opened the door and put on the stove and oven for us. He helped the girls out of their coats and gloves, and he rubbed their hands while they stood in front of the oven. I thought Christian should have made this run himself.

Soon, winter now gone and summer was here. Walking through the apartment complex on my way to the mailbox, I ran into this tall slim Caucasian man as he was getting his mail. We spoke, and out of curiosity, I asked him if he owned a truck. I never had a problem approaching someone and asking questions.

Petite Breaux

"Yes, I have a truck. What do you need?"

"How much would you charge to move my furniture?"

He quoted a price I could not afford.

"Is there any furniture that you could use?" I asked.

I did not have that kind of money and would trade some furniture for the move. He had a one-bedroom apartment with no bed. I had a queen-size headboard and footboard with side rails in excellent shape. I had a nice mattress, too. He was more than happy to accept my offer. Plans were set in motion. We agreed! All the while, things were going good at home. I was keeping Christian happy and satisfied, for a while at least. Anything could set him off quickly.

I did not tell anyone what I was up to because I did not want anyone to slip up and tell Christian. I had found myself an apartment across the street and up the road, not far, but I had to go where rent was affordable. I put down my deposit, and my plan was to move everything out while Christian was at work. I knew he would become extremely angry with this one. Everything was mine, furniture and all. The kids would be in school, and I had someone to move me. I was thrilled and scared at the same time, fearing Christian would probably try to kill me.

Christian was becoming jealous of me having a real, paying job and that I was making more than he was. Timing was everything. I had set things in motion. That time of year was when the kids would be gone for the summer. I kept going to work and acting as if all was normal. I put a deposit down on the new apartment at Treehouse and set a date for the move, which was only two weeks away. I called Francine to tell her of my plans.

"Why don't you just move back to The Parrish?" she asked.

"No, I can't. I want to make it on my own. Everything will be okay."

I loved Christian, or so I thought. We were young and did not know the meaning of real love. Love to us was physical and sexual attraction.

I was still stressing at work, trying to pass my coding. I had only a few hours remaining. I could not focus. I could not think. I was in a terrible state of mind. That's when my manager came to me and said, "Your husband had been coming up here, checking to see if you're here. It's a problem." Now with more to worry about, I was trying to pass my coding while wondering about Christian jeopardizing my job and stalking me.

Time went by and the time had come to move into my new apartment. Christian was at work, and the girls were in The Parrish with Francine. Melik stayed with my friend while I worked. I talked to the person who was to move me, and he was ready. They started moving things around eight o'clock that morning. It only took one trip, and my new place was less than a mile away. I continued working and catching rides. I had two more hours left of coding, and I had to pass to be hired on permanently.

At this time, I didn't know what was going on with Christian or how he might react to my moving out without him knowing. I was sure in my mind that he would be furious and look for me. I had had enough of Christian and his beatings. I was neither his child nor his punching bag.

My younger cousins wanted to come for a visit. They lived in Oleander City, and I thought it'd be fun. There were four of them, ages ranging from around seven to the early teens. About a week later, my cousins were there, all settled in. I was still working and had one more hour of coding to pass.

I came home one day to find Christian at my new place. He was sitting in the living room, all calm, or so it seemed. The reason could have been that my cousins were there.

Looking around, he asked why I had left. I explained that I had to, that I could not take any more of his abuse or have my children scared and upset. He was jeopardizing my employment. I could not be seen with busted lips and bruises. I asked him to leave, and he did with no complaint. This was much scarier than when he had shown signs of anger. He was too calm—the storm was coming.

A couple of days went by, and I was working on my last coding hour. I did not complete it in time, and I was devastated. My manager came to me and explained that time had run out. I was not going to be able to continue working there. I cried and asked the manager to give me more time to complete the coding. What was I going to do? I had no money, just moved and no car. My thoughts were all over the place.

I had no way home, and I was let go early. Diesel did not get off until eleven o'clock, and it was then about eight o'clock. Diesel said he could take me home on his lunch break if I could wait. *Hell, what other choice did I have?* I lived about fifteen minutes from the job. I could wait.

I had one more paycheck owed to me. Until then, I would have to start looking for a new job and figure things out before summer was over and it was time for the kids to return.

A couple of days passed. I had a phone call from Diesel.

"How are you doing? Do you need anything?"

"Everything is fine; I just need to get a few groceries."

I had nothing in the kitchen, and company was coming in from out of town.

"I can take you to the store." He said.

He also told me that some friends from work were going out bowling later and asked if I wanted to tag along.

" Okay, but I did not have the money to bowl."

Diesel agreed to pay for me to bowl, and that evening around three, Diesel came to pick me up. While sitting at the traffic light, Christian and I locked eyes. He was sitting outside in front of his friend's apartment. I could see something trigger in him, and, next thing you know, the light had changed and Christian was running toward the car in the middle of traffic, chasing the car barefoot. I said nothing.

Diesel had not noticed Christian until he caught up with us. Traffic was moving too slow, and my heart was beating too fast. I was praying the light would change sooner, that traffic would move faster, and that Diesel and I could just be on our way without any trouble. The pounding on the trunk of Diesel's car startled him. Diesel looked through his mirror.

"What the fuck? Is that your husband? Do you want me to pull over so you two can talk? I don't have time for this shit."

Diesel looked over at me and saw how scared I was. "It'll be okay," he assured me nothing would happen to me while he was there.

Diesel pulled off the road into a gas station. Then Christian ran up on the driver's side of the car and threw a punch at Diesel through the window. This made Diesel angry.

"I do not have time to be fighting," Diesel said, getting out of the car to face Christian.

"What is your problem?"

Christian said, "You have my wife in your car."

"I'm a friend and co-worker," Diesel said. "I'm just taking her to the store."

Christian, hothead as usual, pushed Diesel in the chest hard enough to make Diesel stagger. Diesel pushed Christian back, then turned toward the car hurriedly and put one hand under the car seat, searching for his gun. It was not there; he had left it at home. I was relieved the gun was not there. Things would have gone wrong, and someone would have been hurt badly. I was so scared I did not move and just stayed in the car. Diesel got back in the car. Christian raised both hands as if to say, "It's okay for now," and he turned and started running back toward his apartment as if he had something in mind.
This situation could have been handled differently.

Diesel and I continued to the store, and later that evening, we met up with everyone else at the bowling alley. For a moment, I had forgotten all my troubles and actually enjoyed myself. It was a good night. This night, I could relax; it was much needed.

On the way back home, I thanked Diesel for everything. When turning into the apartment complex and passing the pool area, I got a glimpse of someone relaxing on one of the lounge chairs. I was not sure, but in my mind, it was Christian. I did not mention this to Diesel, but on approaching my apartment building, someone came out of nowhere and slammed on Diesel's car hood. Diesel had to slam on the brakes. It was Christian. Diesel did not stop the car completely but came to a slowing pace and kept moving the car toward Christian.

Christian continued slamming on the hood of the car and backing up. Diesel said he was not going to let me out of the car while Christian was enraged and that, again, he did not have time to be in the middle of this mess. He didn't like how it would look for him. He said he would take me to the 7-Eleven convenience store that was on the corner. From there, I could call the police.

This is what he did, and he left, heading home. He promised to contact me the next day.

I got out of the car, went straight to the pay phone, and called the police. I explained what was going on and decided not to wait for them there. *What if Christian followed us and found me alone at the store?* I would be helpless.

I decided to run behind the store and cut through all of the other apartment buildings that led to my apartment complex, which was a good distance. Some apartments had fences six feet high. Some had iron rod fencing around them. I didn't care.

I ran. I climbed over fences. On some, I stood on air conditioning units to get a boost so that I could climb over the fence. I just kept running and climbing as fast as I could. I had no idea where Christian was, but I knew he was not where I was. I was tired, and my flesh was stinging and burning from the scrapes and bruises left over from climbing the fences.

Finally, I made it to my apartment and banged on the door for my cousins to open. Once the door opened, I quickly went in, closed it, and locked it. I explained what was going on and told each of them to get something in case Christian came back to the apartment. Melik was frightened by my reactions. I sat him on the couch and told him not to move. One cousin had an iron frying pan. The other two had iron pots, and I had the wooden broom. We just stood at the front door waiting. I called the police again to make sure they were still en route. They said they were on their way. I was impatiently thinking, *What is taking them so long?*

Christian banged on the door, shouting, "Is Simone in there?"

"No!" my cousins said in panicky voices.

He didn't believe them. He kept knocking on the door and turning the knob. They were all set for him. If he came in, they were going to jump him and beat him with the pots and pans. While holding steady at the front door, they heard a loud crash.

Christian had come through the entire glass window frame. He smashed into the hall wall and put a big dent in it.

Once up off the floor, he threw at me the porcelain duck that was sitting on a table in the hallway. He then charged straight at me.

My cousins had all fled out the front door, or all that was left of it. They left behind on the floor the frying pan and pots they had been holding.

What more could you expect from them? They were scared shitless, and they ran, leaving Melik in the apartment with me. Once Christian reached me, he started throwing punches with everything he had.

He just continued beating me in the face. I was screaming for Christian to stop, screaming for someone to help me. "Help me, somebody, please!" I was scared for Melik, who was crying and yelling out of fear, seeing his mother beaten by someone he loved.

Christian looked as if he were possessed. Nothing was stopping him. I felt I was going to die. I could not take any more hits to the head or face. I felt sick and nauseous. I drifted in and out, my body went limp, my eyesight blurred. I felt faint. I could not see anything. Blood flowed down my face. My eyes closed and I saw stars.

I could hear the neighbors. "Someone help her. Someone stop him."

I had on a cotton baby blue top and pants outfit, which was now a red outfit. I managed to get up slowly to my feet, my legs weak and wobbly. I grabbed my baby and ran into the bathroom. I stood in the bathtub with Melik in front of me, hoping this would stop Christian.

Christian kept shouting at me to put Melik down. Melik was hysterical and didn't want me to hold him. He wanted me to let go. He wanted to go to Christian. At that moment, Melik was afraid of me. He did not know this woman, so badly beaten and unrecognizable with all the blood. The poor child was terrified.

I kept whispering to Melik, "I have you. I have you, Melik. It's okay." I could not hold up much longer. I had been beaten in the head and face uncountable times. I had to put Melik down. I needed to lie down. Just as I did, the police came to the front door.

Christian ran to the front door to talk to the police officer. I lay on the bathroom floor, tired, weak, and nauseous. I overheard the police ask, "Does anyone know who had done this? Where'd they go?" Christian told them that the guy took off down the street.

They were not aware that I was still in the apartment. I managed to yell out a call for help. Hellllpp! Back here! When the police officer came to my side, I told him in a weak, soft voice that Christian was lying and that he was the one who had done this to me.

The police immediately handcuffed him. Another officer ran to where I was lying on the floor, bleeding from the face and head. Christian told the police that he was a preacher.

The police officer that was tending to me was trying to keep me alert and awake until the paramedics arrived. I just kept saying in a slow, soft, and shattered voice that I was tired, nauseous, and that I just wanted to go to sleep. The police officer continued talking to me and telling me that I could not go to sleep, to stay awake. The paramedics arrived, examined me briefly, and then moved me into the living room.

Once propped up in a chair, they checked my eyes, head, neck, and face. The paramedic asked if I felt what he was doing. I said no. He was tapping on a bone protruding out of my nose. He then asked if I had been hit in the face with a pipe or other object. I said, groggily, no, that my estranged husband had hit me several times with a closed fist.

I overheard one of the officers say that this was a crime of passion. They took Christian away in handcuffs while he was still saying that he was a preacher. The paramedics put me on a board, then in a neck brace, and then onto the stretcher.

Once on the stretcher, they continued to tell me to stay with them and not to go to sleep. I do not remember anything else from the ambulance ride.

I woke up in the hospital with a bright light flashing in my face. It was cold in the room. I had all kinds of X-rays taken of my upper body. (See Christian was good at always aiming for my face).

I had to have the bone that was sticking out of my nose shaved down and put back in place. My mandible was a little off, and I had stitches and headgear to wear. They released me after about six or more hours.

A nurse told me someone had called the hospital asking about my condition and left a phone number for me to call once released. The nurse said she had contacted my friends, and they were sending a cab to pick me up.

I left the hospital with several prescriptions to be filled. I did not know who the friends were, where my cousins were, and where Melik was. I did not know where this cab would be taking me. I was in so much pain. I never looked in the mirror to see what I looked like. I just wanted to go home.

The cab took me to my apartment, but I could not enter it. It was roped off with yellow police ribbon, and the windows that Christian had smashed were boarded. While standing there, I wondered where the children were. *Where was I supposed to go? What was I going to do?*

A young man approached and said he had sent the cab to pick me up. It turned out that he was my neighbor, about two doors down. He was not home at the time of the incident but had heard about it. He told me that all the children were at his place. He asked how I was feeling and if I had everything I needed. Whatever I needed he would take care of it for me. He also said the kids and I could stay at his place until we could gain access to my apartment again. I went with him to his place.

My choices were no choices at the time. Once inside his apartment, I found he had a brother, a wife, and one small child living with him. My cousins were sitting on the floor with Melik. I went to pick Melik up, but he struggled away. He knew the voice, but the bandages frightened him. My cousins were all okay but ready to go home. My youngest cousin was about seven years old.

He tried to make light of things and tell me a joke about my porcelain duck. "When Christian threw that duck at me, it said, quack!" Funny, but not funny. He was scared by all the excitement.

The neighbors got my medicine and made sure everyone was fed and comfortable. I knew now that any job searching was out. I had to rethink my plans. I finally contacted my family about what had taken place. They had already heard, but had not heard from me and were worried.

Later, I found out that Christian had to wear hand splints. He had broken both hands while striking me. My family and Christian's family had been feuding about what had happened. Each side made threats, but it was all talk, thank goodness. No need to add more fuel to the fire.

I had had enough of family interference and drama in my life.

Zeike, Christian's friend, had bailed him out of jail, with no charges against him. I wanted to file charges and did, but nothing came of it because we were still married. The laws had not changed yet on domestic violence. There were no state authorities to take over and file charges against Christian.

Christian's family immediately sent for him and moved him back home. Of course, Christian had told them a lie again, his version of what had happened, putting it all on me. He had them so fooled they thought that I was going to get Christian killed or in trouble.

My cousins went back home, and I had to go back into my apartment, where I did not want to stay. It was bloody as hell, a bloodbath from the living room, to the hallway, to the bedroom, and back to the bathroom. The carpet was ruined. I had nowhere else to go at this time.

I called my mother and told her not to bring the girls back. I had to make other arrangements. It was Melik and I alone in the apartment.

I cleaned the apartment as much as I could. The apartment people fixed the window, and they sent someone to clean the carpet.

After about three weeks, I received a notice to vacate the apartment.

Melik still did not want to come to me.

The bandages now removed, but my face was unrecognizable, almost like the *Elephant Man*, with discoloration of dark purple and black, along with much swelling. Finally, I looked in the mirror, and all I could do was cry. I did not think my face would ever heal. I had not been outdoors since the incident. All was lost. I could not do anything more in Saxton. It was time to leave.

I called my grandmother in Oleander City and asked her to come get me. I put all the furniture in storage.

I called a cousin in Oleander City and asked if the kids and I could stay with her for a while.

Slightly Bruised and A Little Broken

While I was getting things in order to put in storage, a girlfriend of mine stopped by. She had heard what had happened and wanted to see how I was doing. If you ever saw the movie *As Good As It Gets* with Jack Nicholson, Cuba Gooding Jr., Greg Kinnear, and Helen Hunt, the Greg Kinnear character was badly beaten, and they all went to the hospital to see him. When Cuba's character enters the hospital room, he cannot keep his composure because of the damage to Greg's face. Cuba acts like a fool. Well, this was my girlfriend, and she said to me that Christian really "fucked you up."

All I could say to her was thank you for that information.

My grandmother was always there for me. She came to get Melik and me the next week. Guess who was behind the steering wheel? Christian.

My grandmother had asked Christian to drive her down to get me.

My grandmother was very forgiving, like no other. I didn't have much to say to Christian. I just got myself together, and we headed back to Oleander City. Christian was apologetic. I wasn't ready for apologies or anything else that Christian had to offer.

I had Francine bring the girls to Oleander City to my cousin's home, where we would stay for a while.

While staying with my cousin, I had to get my nose fixed. I had a deviated septum that was causing me some breathing problems.

I had to have nose surgery.

Petite Breaux

Once the surgery was over, the hospital had given me too much anesthesia, and I could not be woken. It took me a while longer in the recovery room. Christian's sister, her husband, and Christian's brother were great. They had me stay at their home after the surgery. They took good care of me. It was rough after the surgery. I had to sleep sitting up while breathing out of my mouth. Christian's entire family was wonderful—an awesome family. When Christian and I Married they accepted the kids and I into their family as one of their own without judgement.

All better, I went back home to my cousins. I went on government assistance until I could find a job. I found us an apartment.

After about two months, I got a permanent job working with a paper company. I worked the evening shift. I didn't have anyone to watch the kids at night while I worked, so I had to take the chance at leaving them home alone. The kids were young, Sharmayne was ten, Cecilia was eight, and Melik was four years of age. I was always worried about them being home alone, but they were good kids. They stayed in their rooms and they weren't all over the house, but this was a lot on Sharmayne, being the oldest having to tend to her siblings. I would leave to go to work right when they were all coming home from school and didn't return home until after everyone was asleep. This is something I had to do. I had no one to stay with them at the time and I had to work. Things were going good for the most part.

Christian was working his way back in, and I let him. After all that had happened and all that

Christian had put me through, I still loved him. I guess I did not have enough strength, and I knew everyone would talk. It was not for everyone to like my decision but to support it. Love can be blind at any cost. It was a very stupid move on my part, but I wanted to give it one last try.

Maybe Christian would change. Christian moved in with the kids and me.

A few months after that, Francine moved back to Oleander City, and she moved in with us. Things were fine in the beginning, but then Francine and Christian were at odds, and it was a tug-of-war for me. They were pulling me from each end. I was miserable from being put in the middle of those two. I began to have stomach problems. I eventually ended up at the doctors. I was told that I was a worrier and that this was causing my stomach to tighten in knots. The doctor said if I did not tell each of them how I felt, my condition would worsen.

My doctor said to tell my mother that I was not going to listen to her talk about her husband, and if she felt strongly about it, she needed to move. "I know you love your mother and she will always be your mother, but you need to be treated in a respectful manner." The same thing went for Christian.

Now, back at home, I was approached by Francine. "Let me know what you plan on doing: staying with your husband or leaving him? If he stays, then I'm leaving."

"You are my mother, and this is my husband, and you are not going to make me choose between the two. I am not going to ask Christian to leave just because that is what you want."

Francine decided it would be best for her to move. Christian stayed but not much longer. I was tired and knew the marriage wasn't going to work. Christian was up to his old tricks of cheating, so I divorced him.

When I went to the lawyer's office, he asked, "What do you want from the divorce?"

"Only my maiden name," I said, because Christian had made the threat that I was his as long as I had his last name.

His mother had told me what Christian said. "I love her so much it makes my heart hurt."

My thoughts on that? I don't need that kind of love.

"How soon do you want to get started with the filing?" the lawyer asked.

"I don't have the money now. What is the fee?"

"I tell you what, you can pay me later. Let us just get it over with."

And so we did. I got my maiden name back and have not seen or talked to Christian since.

I continued to work at the paper company for a while longer.

After the first punch to the face, it should have been warning enough to say enough. No, not me, not that girl.

Now this will never happen again. Loving someone does not mean physically or verbally abusing him or her. I should not have left the state with my children to move to another state where we knew no one. They had to endure everything I went through. My struggle was their struggle. I made the choice to uproot us and move, and they suffered the consequences of my actions. They should have never had to witness so much violence. I never thought how this would affect them emotionally within their lives. I believed that they would be okay, but along the way, I started noticing little things, such as Sharmayne biting her nails all the time, Melik's growing anger issues, and Cecilia was different. It was if nothing bothered her either way.

Although I did not let anything happen to them physically, I failed them emotionally.

Petite Breaux

~ Twelve ~
WHO SAID THE GRASS WAS GREENER

Darwin and I began dating when I was about twenty-seven years of age. A coworker of mine, who was also a friend of Darwin, was having a party at her home. This is how Darwin and I met. We developed a relationship that went on for about two years. Darwin moved in with the kids and me. Darwin was a good provider. He worked nights and I worked days.

Problem number one was Darwin was on a bowling league, which took up his weekends.

Problem number two was I decided I needed a hobby, something to occupy those times when he was not available for us.

Problem number three was we had some shady, underhanded interference from associates of Darwin who were trying to come between us. I give credit to Darwin for handling the situation like a man.

****

Petite Breaux

"Does anybody want to take art lessons?" I asked the kids.

"I do," Melik said.

"I guess," Cecilia said.

"No, I don't want no part of it," Sharmayne said.

So, the three of us started taking lessons three times a week. This worked out great for a while, but I realized Darwin and I still weren't spending any time together. I talked to him about it, and he said he would give me Saturdays for us.

Nevertheless, it did not happen; he had bowling and then the boys. I began to get close to my art instructor,

Scott, and I started talking outside of class. At this time, I was not giving Darwin a second thought. My attention was elsewhere.

I guess Darwin's intuition kicked in, and he proposed to me. I refused because I felt it was for all the wrong reasons.

"Okay," he said. "I'll ask again one day."

Well, that day never came, and I became more involved elsewhere. My relationship with Darwin was over. He moved out, and that was it for us. You know what they say: the grass is greener on the other side. Well, I sure thought it was, but found out very soon that the grass had weeds all throughout it.

The excitement I felt with Scott was not the excitement I needed. Scott had relationships going with others from the classes he taught. I confronted him, and I was not satisfied with his answers. I decided to tell his father what was going on. *Why did I* do that? His father set up a meeting with me at the office. I thought it would be he and I only. I called a cab to get to the meeting. Cecilia and Melik were with me. While sitting in Scott's father's office explaining to him what was going on with Scott and me, here enters Scott. Immediately my thoughts were, what is he doing here? His dad had told him to come to the office and explain his side. After hearing what I had to say, Scott became furious! The chair that I sat in, he picked it up off the floor with me still sitting in it and tossed it across the floor. This frightened Melik and he ran out the door outside of the building and just kept running around the building frantically.

As I lay on the floor inside, Scott knelt down side of me with fist drawn back, Cecilia shouts out "SCOTT NO! Scott looked at Cecilia and backed away. He assaulted me right in front of his father, who did nothing. I gathered my children and we left.

Scott later came to my apartment and assaulted me again by punching me in my arms and thighs. I contacted the police.

We had a court date, and Scott made me look very stupid. He had convinced one of the other students to lie for him and say that I received the bruises while in class when something fell on me. I thought this man must have been paying people off to lie for him. Even some of those on the police force changed their stories. The judge ruled the case self-inflicted and dismissed it.

Are you fucking kidding me?

I had contacted some of the girls and women from the class to discuss Scott. I contacted everyone I could reach that I thought Scott had been involved with. Once he got wind of my actions, he set me up real good, taking measured steps so I could not bring him down. He would call my home phone and hang up, knowing that I would call him back. Doing this, he established phone logs that I called him. Unaware that he was recording our conversations, he would say things that would make me mad and I would answer harshly, which came across as threats. He would ask me to join him to visit some of his friends, so I went.

Later, I'd get another court date in the mail. I saw these same friends in the hall of the courthouse and I did not have a clue as to why they were there. Later, an attorney came out of the courtroom. She talked to us both and advised me to quit stalking Scott or harassment charges would be filed against me. If you could have seen my face, I was just dumbfounded. I had no clue as to what the lawyer was talking about. *What did I do?*

The attorney said if we could just both stay away from one another, then there would be no need to further the case. I just said yes, that I agreed to stay away from him. Then, I realized that his friends were there to support him if needed, to say that I had been with him, as if I had followed him those nights when we all went out.

Scott had convinced me that I was the only person he was dating, and for the life of me, I had no reason to doubt him. When he wasn't teaching lessons, he was at my place. He said I acted as if he had fourteen hours in a day. He was smooth, very smooth, and he covered his ass. I wanted revenge.

Scott had been doing his dirt and getting away with it. I talked to a friend of mine whom I worked with and told him what had happened. He did not like what I was telling him. Later, I heard a rumor that vandals had demolished Scott's car. *Go figure!* It seems someone else got to him before I did. (Chuckle.)

~ Thirteen ~
WHY PAY FOR THE COW?

I moved to Stanton in 1995. I dated, I moved around, and after about two years, I was shopping around for a car when I met Merrick, who worked in the financing department of a car dealership. Merrick rode with me as I took a car on a test drive, and we continued our conversation in the car.

Once we completed all the paperwork for the car, we exchanged phone numbers. We never went out on a real date. I went up to the dealership a couple of times after closing hours where we would have dinner in his office. Merrick would come to my place from time to time.

This went on for about a year, but it was nothing to brag about. He never promised me anything. He never said he was leaving his wife, and I didn't want him to. I wasn't into him that way.

He did say that he and his wife were not intimate because she had bad back problems. I was getting tired that I could not call him when I wanted to, nor could I see him when I wanted to. I hated that we never went out together anywhere. I finally realized that I was nothing but a sex toy for him, and he was not doing anything for me. Like they say: why buy the cow when you can have the milk free?

Well, I was free milk!

I needed help paying my rent, so I called Merrick. "Can you help me pay my rent this month?" I asked.

"Do I look like I do charity cases?" Merrick replied.

That was it. I was done with Merrick, so I slammed the phone down on the receiver. I could not believe he had said that to me. I had bought him a Christmas gift and a birthday gift when I should have been spending that money on my children's needs. I was hurt and crushed.

I regretted ever getting involved with this married man. I knew then that I meant nothing to this person, and he was just using me for his pleasure. Chalk it up as another lesson learned.

I met Eric at the same dealership as Merrick. Eric was a new hire. We started talking and went out on a date. Eric was a talker. He talked a good game and I fell for it. He lived at home with his mother and brother. I was still involved with Merrick somewhat while I involved myself with Eric.

Eric decided one day to come over with more clothes than he needed for one night. I did not say anything at the time. I just wanted to see where all this was going.

Eric needed a ride home from work one evening. I told him I would pick him up. What he didn't know was that I was going to see Merrick before picking him up. While fooling around with Merrick, I lost track of time and was late picking up Eric.

The building had closed, so he was waiting outside. I told him I was sorry for being late, and that was that, but you could tell he was upset. Heck, I would be too. There is nothing like getting off work and your ride is not there after you have rushed to get outside.

We got home, and I was in the bed with Eric when the phone rang. It was Merrick. While I was on the phone with Merrick, Eric was lying next to me, either awake or asleep. I did not know because I did not check.

"I'm just checking to see if you made it home okay?"

I said yes but with short, hurried answers.

"Why do you sound like you have a cold?"

"Oh, it's just because of the way I'm lying down." I continued talking to Merrick, and neither Merrick nor Eric was any wiser than the next. I finished our conversation and hung up. I went to work the next day with a hickey on my neck and tried to keep it covered so that Merrick would not see it. After work that evening, I asked Eric if he had any money he could give toward the bills. After all, we had just been paid.

"I don't have any money left because I have to pay my mother rent and other bills," he said.

That night, while Eric was sleeping, I slithered out of bed, crawled around on the floor, got his wallet out of his pants pocket, and eased myself to the restroom very quietly. I opened his wallet and saw that he had seven hundred dollars in it.

I took two hundred, crawled back on the floor to his pants, put the wallet back in his pocket, and then, I crawled back into bed. I lay there thinking how he had lied to me and how I was feeling stupid again because I had asked for help and been turned down.

I thought that maybe I should tell these men what I needed instead of asking for what I wanted. Maybe I would have gotten the help I needed. I was upset, and I slithered out of bed again and did the same routine. I crawled to Eric's pants, got the wallet out, went into the bathroom, and took another two hundred from his wallet. I crawled back to his pants, put the wallet back in, and slid myself back into bed.

Finally, I was satisfied and went to sleep.

I awoke extra early the next morning. I quietly got up out of bed, got dressed and tiptoed out of the apartment. I got into my car, drove to the bank, and deposited the four hundred dollars into my account.

I returned home, eased back into the apartment and back into bed, and I went back to sleep. I was happy because I could pay my rent and other bills. I had my check, but I was just short. I got up to go to work as usual. I left before Eric awoke and headed to work.

When Eric got to work, he asked, "Did you take any money out of my wallet?"

"No."

When I got home that evening, my son told me that Eric had asked him and his friend if they had taken money out of his wallet. Eric had no idea what had happened to his money. (He does now.)

It was the weekend and Eric was out with the fellas. He came home around one or two in the morning, pissy drunk. I was in bed asleep. I heard him go into the restroom, but something sounded strange, so I got up to find that he had pissed all over my bathroom floor and all into my dirty clothes basket. The floor was flooded, and he got into bed as if it was nothing. I tried to wake him up. I was angry and shouting, "Get your nasty, pissy ass up and out of here right now, and don't come back." I think I just needed an excuse. I was tired of him and angry at how he lied to me about not being able to help with the bills.

I was starting to see a pattern here: you bring up money and you can find out quickly who is sincere about you and who is not.

Slightly Bruised and A Little Broken

~ Fourteen ~
COULD THIS BE MY SOUL MATE?

I was working at this retail store in Stanton, and Wallace would come in on occasions. He would try to strike up a conversation with me. I thought he was just bothering me, so I would always give him a hard time. On top of that, I was not interested. He was persistent, so I gave in.

Wallace and I had so much in common, but we were so different in other ways. We both loved to read books. We did not like the club scene. We did not smoke, but we both drank wine and wine coolers. We liked movies and eating out. He became my comfort zone. I just was not attracted to him in the beginning. He was not, what we say, my type. Exactly what is a type?

We have this image in our minds of what we want, whom we want, and what we are looking for in someone, but do we ever really get it? The exterior of a person rather than the interior consumes us. The true essence of a person is what is on the inside. The exterior can fool us and break out hearts. I always wanted a tall man, about six feet or taller, of medium build with an athletic physique, someone with strong facial features who laughed a lot.

Who was I kidding? He never came along.

What I got after years of wrong men was Wallace, who was not six feet but had all the qualities of what a real man should be. After about three months of dating, I realized that I never actually was with someone that I would consider my type. Therefore, this "type" thing seemed to be a wish list, something we would like to have but cannot find or get.

Wallace had qualities that I longed for. He was nice, soft-spoken, and a true man. He treated me with respect, something I had not had from anyone. He cared for me and about me. He would always cook me breakfast and dinner, making sure that I ate. If I need financial help he was there no questions asked, but I still tried to hold my own without asking. It was wonderful. He was spoiling me, and this had become my comfort zone. I just knew. I was sure I had finally found my soul mate. I could breath a little easier.

Wallace would come over to the house all the time with his chips, salsa, Oreo cookies, and a Coke, and we would sit and watch a movie. When we were not at the house, we would go out to the movies, dinner, comedy shows, and take weekend trips from time to time, though these trips were infrequent.

Wallace worked a part-time job some evenings. I would go to his place and spend the night, but we were not connecting. Something was off; we were not clasping together. We continued dating, but one night,

I just decided I was not into him anymore. So, while sitting in the car, waiting to go inside to a comedy show, I told Wallace the truth. "I just want to let everything go. I'm not feeling us."

"Can you give it more time?" Wallace asked. "Let your guard down and things might change for you."

I gave it some thought, and said, "Okay."

Wallace was not always available. Even on the nights he did not work the second job, he said that he needed some time for himself. This made me upset because it seemed odd. I understood needing some "me" time, but sometimes his "me" time was out with someone else.

I did not want to see other people while dating him, and I knew we each said that we were not looking for a relationship. This was another reason we should keep sex out of dating. Intimacy changes things, so we look for more than what the other person is willing to offer.

Wallace was still involved with his ex-girlfriend, and I found out he was involved with a few other young women he had been seeing.

After about one year of dating, my lease was up at the house where I was staying, and Wallace and I decided that I would move in with him. At this same time, I told Cecilia that it was time for her to move out on her own, and I asked Melik to move with Wallace and me. Melik did not want to go. I asked Cecilia, my middle daughter, to let him move in with her and be his guardian.

Cecilia rented a small two-bedroom apartment on the opposite side of town where Melik could continue to attend school and be near his friends. After six months, Cecilia was tired of being on her own. She took a Greyhound bus and moved back to Oleander City to live with her grandmother Francis.

Sharmayne then took over the apartment with Melik.

Wallace told me to let my shield down. He knew that I was used to running my household by myself but that I should let him be the man. He would say, "You do not have to be in that survivor mode any longer. I got you!"

After all was moved and settled in, we were having great times. Wallace's female friends were calling the house phone. He would answer and hold conversations. I found this to be rude. I had answered the phone on different occasions and ended up in arguments with the ex-girlfriend and another young girl. His ex had the nerve to ask me why I was answering Wallace's phone, that I was just his roommate, so I explained it.

"Honey! I am more than just a roommate."

I guess Wallace told her we were nothing but roommates. Wallace thought it was okay to stay connected with his exes, but I didn't, so I told him how I felt. "If you do not have children with these women, then an ex should remain just that: an ex." I should not have to argue with these women. It was

Wallace's responsibility to get them in check. Something was not right with this.

Wallace and I argued about this, and he told me that I would never be someone that he would consider marrying. I let this man get me to the lowest point in my life, and I tried to take it. After that conversation, I vowed I would never again let anyone get me to such a low point. I was stronger than that and had survived much worse.

About ten months later, Wallace was offered a job in Hamilton. I would remain in the home until Wallace found someone to rent the house. Wallace and I would see each other about every other weekend.

Wallace was a good person. He was there for me whenever I needed him, day or night. One day, my car broke down, and he had me drive him back to Hamilton so that I could keep his car while my car was being repaired. He would take public transportation to work. He did things like this all the time, not just for me, but also for others. He made many sacrifices with no complaints. Things were going great, or so I thought, but I quickly found out we were not on the same page.

With Wallace down the road, I would always try to keep the relationship exciting, even after he moved to another state. He would come home on weekends, and I would have a different theme set up for us. I was a romantic. I would have a beach theme one week, and I would wrap myself up in wrapping paper from neck to toe with a bow on my head and with nothing underneath.

Moments like this went on for a few months, and then the house was rented out. I moved into my own place.

Melik came back to live with me in the townhouse. Our relationship remained okay, but Melik was misbehaving and getting on my nerves.

I was to have surgery, and Wallace came to town to be there with me. He took good care of me. I had foot surgery, so I had to wear a shoe boot on both feet, and I could not walk.

On Halloween night, I was lying in my bed when I heard Melik running up and down the stairs, hysterical, crying, and shouting, "Oh my God, oh my God."

Of course, this got me all hysterical. I didn't know what in the hell this boy had gotten ahold of, acting all crazy. I tried to get out of bed to ask him what was going on. *He took off down the stairs, saying, "I saw something outside the window on the roof."*

"What?" I asked, but he just left the house and left me. I was standing there afraid, yelling for Melik to come back. I went to my bedroom, locked my door, and got underneath my covers. I was so scared—of what, I didn't know. That was the problem. I didn't know what this boy saw, or if he saw anything.

Later that night, I thought I heard something or someone in the kitchen downstairs, and it wasn't Melik. I got my cell phone, hid in the closet, and called the police. I was told to stay there until they said it was all clear. They came and checked around the townhouse, found nothing, and I came out of the closet. My feet were hurting. I was walking on my heels.

That damn Melik. I didn't know what was going on with him. I thought, He done got hold of some bad drugs or something.

The next day I contacted Wallace and told him what had happened and that Melik was not reliable enough to take care of me. I could not get downstairs like I needed to.

Wallace said he would come get me and take me back to his place until I recovered. Wallace was an excellent caregiver. I could not ask for anyone better. I believe me being at his place caused him to change some plans he may have had with someone else. He did not mention it, but I knew.

I returned home after a week and went back to work.

Time passed, and then a change came over Wallace. He started acting distant—you know how they do when they are up to something wrong and nothing we can say or do is ever right. They pick little petty arguments to leave or get away. I wasn't dumb. I knew the signs, and I was one to do my research. I didn't need anyone to tell me anything about what Wallace was doing or not doing.

I needed my own facts and proof.

Wallace, when he came home on weekends, said my show of affection was too much, that he could not breathe, and that I was smothering him. Yep, he had met up with some old chick who had found him and started emailing him. He was driving down the road during the week to visit her and take her out to dinner and to see a comedy show. He even loaned her money because she said she was a struggling model. I thought he was being stupid and that all she wanted him for was money. He never got it back. He wasn't sure if he should continue seeing this girl. Would she be too much drama for him? He was quiet and did not like drama. I do not know how he ended it, but he did. I never let on that I knew about this. We had stopped talking once he said I was smothering him. He pushed me away. I was hurt, but I had to move on. I didn't have time to mope. Yep, he came back and I accepted him.

    I do not know what it was with him and me. I do know we helped each other, but this was not my first time dealing with Wallace and his other young women. He did not want a relationship with any of them, just sex. He was the type to treat you right, wine and dine you, cook for you, just a do-right-by-you kind of person. This treatment and behavior can be misleading for all involved. He could not see it. He could be somewhat naïve at times. He did not want a relationship with anyone, truth be told, not even with me.

    That was my fault, going from not feeling him to falling hard too fast. We had only been seeing each other about four months, so I did not give it a second thought. We both went into this saying we were not looking for a relationship. It was still early, and no one said anything about monogamous dating. He said he had been dating about four times a month, but he was secretive about it.

You know how when you call someone on the phone and they try to sound asleep or they ask you questions, like how your day was, sounding like a business call or something. At the time,

I was in night classes, studying to become a medical assistant. I would call him once I got home. One particular night, I called, and he was speaking to me as if he were talking to his son. He was asking basic questions, such as, "So how was school?" This conversation was odd to me, and then I heard a female in the background. She was not aware that he was on the phone, and she stopped talking abruptly in mid-sentence. It was as if Wallace might have put up a finger, like, "Shh, I'm on the phone."

Yes, I knew all about Wallace's little female secrets that he tried to keep hidden, but how do you keep things hidden when you are someone who writes everything down, such as time, date, and whereabouts? He would keep all this in his black planner, like, *Called Ms. Hathaway.*

Yep, I looked in his planner, sure did. If you do not want to talk to me, I will find out on my own. If we are both doing our own thing, just say I have company right now, but don't try to play me like a fiddle.

Wallace was in his third year living in Hamilton when he asked me to move there with him. With no hesitation, I said that I would. That April of 2004, we loaded up the truck and it was, "Hamilton, here I come." (This was the same year that I found out that I was going to be a grandmother.) We had picked out a nice apartment for us both. I continued working at my job in Stanton. I would commute each day, waking at three in the morning to be out the door by four. I started my shift at six and left work at four in the evening, heading back to Hamilton. Once home, around six or six thirty, I would get myself ready for the next day and do my online school homework. I was taking online classes.

After several months of this, Wallace came to me and said he was feeling neglected. I could understand that, and it did not go unrecognized. I was just tired. I told him I would try to do better. The next month, I resigned from my government job in Stanton so that I could have more time at home with him. I could not handle the long commute any longer anyway. Now I had the stress of looking for employment.

So, the neglect problem continued, and my trying never happened. I got a position at the same company where Wallace worked, and I thought things were going to get better, but it was too late. Wallace had had enough and asked me to leave. I got another apartment up the road, and he stayed the last two months of the lease in our old apartment. Then, he moved into his own apartment in another county.

He was doing his thing, and I was doing what I do best, working and staying at home. This went on for the next two years, but we saw each other from time to time. We had dinner, a movie, whatever. We got along better apart.

Whenever things were not going the way Wallace wanted them to go, he wanted to end the relationship. Whenever I was not who Wallace wanted me to be, he was ready to end it all. Wallace wanted to change me into someone more to his liking. He did not like my character, my openness, things I would say, my actions, and that I had that being-in-control attitude. But it wasn't that I did not want him to take charge. I had been the head of my household for many years. I just could not go soft and trust him with everything, not at that time.

I always told him to quit trying to change me, to let me do it on my own. Forcing me would only make things worse. If I tried to be who he wanted me to be, then I would be faking it. I was not him, nothing like him. I was me.

We grew closer together again, and after six years of being together, Wallace told me that he loved me, and I believed him. He had never said anything even close to how he felt about me in the past. Wallace took a job back in Stanton, and he said he wanted me with him.

Of course I said yes.

We both packed up and moved in two months. This meant quitting my stable employment and relying on Wallace to provide for me until I found a new job. Back in Stanton, during the December of 2007, we moved back into Wallace's house, which he had been renting out in his absence, and I was job-hunting again.

Months later, I got a job that lasted a few months, but then they had a layoff. I was unemployed again, but at least I received unemployment. I got another job at a retail store and remained there until I was selected for a position in Augusta City.

In Augusta City, I worked again for the government. It did not last long, about eight months. I was lied on, lied about, and ended up moving back to Oleander City to my mother's home. Ironically, Wallace was living at my mother's, as he had taken a position in Oleander City.

I was collecting unemployment once again.

Wallace and I really weren't getting along while we were at my mother's home, so we decided it best that he move into his own place.

Wallace was in his place; later, I decided to give him a call, but something was not right. "What are you doing?"

"Cooking."

"Do you have company?"

"Yes."

I hung up the phone. I was upset that he could move on so quickly. In bed that night, I could not sleep, so I put on my jacket, still in my pajamas. I got in the car and drove to Wallace's apartment. I knocked on the door. I could hear him at the door looking through the peephole but not opening the door. I recognized the unfamiliar car in the parking lot, so I knew there was a woman at his apartment.

"Open the door."

He cracked the door about an inch wide.

I tried to push pass him but could not. "Let me in. Let me see who you have in here. Let me see what she looks like. She's probably young."

He came out on the porch, trying to convince me to leave and go home.

I said, "No, I'll leave once your company leaves."

He would not go back inside, so we stood there for about fifteen minutes, and the chick never came outside to see what was going on. He finally said, "She'll leave after you do."

I grew tired, so I left. The next morning I was up early and right back to his apartment. He opened the door, and the girl was gone. I left and went back home. A year later, I accepted a job with the government in Akron. I packed up, moved to Akron, and remained there for four months. Then I was offered another position in Madison Bridge, and Wallace helped me move. After about two years in Madison Bridge, Wallace tried to make a sacrifice and get us under one roof together. He decided, job or no job, that he would move to Madison Bridge where I was.

He was with me a short two weeks when he was offered a job back in Stanton where he remains to date.

~Fifteen~
WRONGFUL TERMINATION

Lied on and lied about for no reason that I could understand, I relocated to Augusta City in 2008 to start my new position within the government. I had accepted the offer previously and was to start that April. I had already found an apartment online, about thirty miles from downtown. It was no different from all my other moves. I knew no one in the state, but I was okay with that. I was used to moving and not knowing anyone. I would eventually meet new people but not get too friendly.

I would familiarize myself with my new surroundings. Once I began the new position, two co-workers and I decided to carpool since we all lived in the same area. This worked out fairly well. It helped

Petite Breaux

on gas. We each took a week at driving. Sometimes one would drive more than a week, and we would all pitch in on gas.

My manager was female. The rumor was that she was a hard-ass and intimidated some people. I did not think anything of it. I did not know her. I was glad to have an income. My thought has always been, do your job, be polite, and show respect, and no worries.

Other rumors about her were that she somehow had several other new hires terminated from their positions before their probation period was reached. See, it is easy to be fired within that year of your probation, but once you make that year and a day, you are in, and it takes an act of God to lose your position, which, by the way, needs to be changed.

Anyhow, I had put in for time off after about a week. I wanted to go home and get my furniture. I was sleeping on an inflatable that was killing my back.

My manager approved my leave, so all was good; I could go get my furniture. One of my co-workers asked if I put in for any leave. I said yes. My co-worker was a mid-twenties woman who had a husband and a family with a newborn baby one month of age in another state. She had taken the same position as I had, but I had no small children of concern. When she accepted the position, her husband could not relocate at that time. She had not seen her family since we started in April. It was now August.

"Have you requested any leave yet?" I asked.

"I did, but was thinking of not taking it," she said.

"Why?"

"Because Miranda scares me, and she is very intimidating."

I explained to her that if you are approved for leave, you have nothing to be concerned about. *(little did I know.)* She needed to take her leave, if not to see her husband, then for her newborn child. I questioned her about why was she afraid of Miranda, the manager.

"Because of the way she looks at me and talks down to me," she said.

I said, "Don't let that frighten you. That fear is what she wants. Just do your job and don't worry about that. You have more concerns going home to visit family and distressing from this place." I told her, "I would not retract my leave. If anything, I would be happy and looking forward to the break." Miranda would talk to employees any kind of way and would get away with it. I noticed this particular agency had a majority of females in high-authority positions.

It was a power struggle. You would constantly hear: I am her boss—just boss, boss, and boss. They all had bad attitudes and did not know how to treat us employees. They were not management material. I am finding out more and more these days that some people do not know how or cannot handle having a title. This environment was made to be miserable.

I took my vacation, and while on leave, I had a missed call from my manager. Miranda, on my voicemail, told me I needed to get back to work, that I was needed. I remember one of my other co-workers telling me that while she was off sick, Miranda kept calling her, saying she needed to get back to work. *What kind of shit was this woman pulling?*

Well, I was dumbfounded, and there was not a damn thing I could do about it. I was over ten hours away. Once I returned to work, my manager asked to see me. We discussed my leave, and she said she did not approve me for leave.

She wasn't going to pay me for the time I took off, and I would be charged with AWOL (absent without leave). I explained to Miranda that she could not do that, that I needed my money. I had just moved there and had an apartment and other bills to pay. She had approved my leave. I retrieved my leave slip, showing her approval. She refused to honor her own approval.

I left the office, and I contacted the union representative. She came across as if she would fight for me. She was acting on my behalf, or at least I thought so. I told her what had happened. She talked to my manager, and my manager said that she would remove the AWOL but still wasn't going to pay me for my time off. I was really upset by all this and could not figure out why this woman was doing this to me.

I was so sick of people lying on me for no apparent reason at all, just blame shifting. I had just left that same type of mess in Stanton with Wallace's sisters and his youngest sister's boyfriend.

I was heading to the restroom when I ran into a woman who worked on another floor. In casual conversation, I told her what was going on between Miranda and me (wrong thing to do). She jokingly said, "You better leave Miranda alone."

I said back to her jokingly, "I have not done anything to Miranda; it's the other way around."

This whole situation was odd to me, because Miranda had always—in the few months I had been working there—called on me to do things for her that were work related. She wanted me to learn certain things pertaining to my position. Miranda said I reminded her of herself with my work ethics (the hard work, not the attitude or intimidation). I was like her miniature self. Even one of my co-workers would joke and call me little Miranda.

One day, Miranda went so far as to ask me to talk to one of my female co-workers about her dress attire. Miranda wanted me to ask her to tone it down and tell her how she needed to be dressing in her work environment. I politely said I could not do that request. I thought something of that nature should come from management, not me. This could put me in a bad situation, not only with my co-worker, but also with upper management. *Who am I to tell someone how to dress?* Miranda said okay. She just thought because my co-worker and I had lunch together that this made us friends.

So, back to the matter at hand. Upon arriving to work the next day, the day after the leave incident, I was early, at my usual time. I was still uneasy because my pay was still unresolved (for me, anyhow). Prior to leaving work that day, Miranda had sent out an email to her staff, saying that she was leaving early for the day. She was not feeling well. As I was saying, I arrived at my usual time: eight forty-five in the morning. I usually beat everyone in, and Miranda usually came in around nine thirty to ten o'clock. This particular morning, I went to my desk, and I saw Miranda's door was open about a foot wide. I didn't look in. I just continued to my desk to put all my stuff down and settled in. I decided to go see if Miranda was in her office because it was early for her to be at work. I peeped in her window. I saw her standing behind her desk, and it appeared as if she was straightening up as if she was about to leave for the day. I stuck my head in the opening of the door. I knocked lightly, a quick rata-tap-tap, "Good morning. Excuse me, Miranda, but can I speak to you for a minute?"

When Miranda looked up at me, I could see something was wrong. Something was bothering her. She had been crying. Before I could say anything else, Miranda snapped at me, "What do you want?"

"Would it be okay if I moved to another area, a different manager?"

I didn't feel it was going to work out for us after yesterday.

Miranda said angrily and quickly, "Do what you want to do, Simone! I don't care."

I shut the door and left. *That did not go so well.* I went to lunch around eleven thirty. After lunch, I went to my desk, and the secretary came to me. When she asked if I was Simone, I said yes.

"Ms. Alexander wants to see you in her office." Ms. Alexander was Miranda's manager.

I thought, *What is this about?*

I got up and went straight to Ms. Alexander's office, and no sooner did I enter her doorway that she started her interrogation. "Did you see Miranda this morning in her office?" No hi, or how are you doing, or anything. Just questions.

"Yes, I did," I said.

Before I could continue on, she cut me off by putting her hand up. "You're fired, immediately. I need you to sign this paper. Go clean out your desk. Leave your badge. On the way out of the courtyard, stop by the guard's desk and have your parking decal removed from your windshield."

"What happened?" I asked.

"Miranda came to me all upset and crying, stating that you came in extra early this morning, kicked her office door in, and started shouting threatening remarks to her. You told her that you had better not catch her outside."

OMG! My jaw dropped, and again, I tried to explain myself.

Miranda's manager said, "I do not want to hear it." She did not want to hear any *he said, she said*. "Just leave."

Miranda had lied about me and gone home for the day. She knew I was on probation and would be terminated. She was good. She had planned this well. *Did I intimidate her because she saw she did not intimidate me?* I was never a threat to Miranda or her position, so why would she react this way toward me? I had no problem with Miranda. I liked her as a person. I did not like the attitude she had with others, but she never had it with me.

I was told this is what she does to get rid of anyone she feels might have the nerve to question her.

I guess she had a reputation to maintain. Miranda would never let anyone confront her and get away with it. My kicking in her door and threatening her would have never gone down.

Miranda probably would have beat my ass that morning. Miranda was at least three times my size. I never could come to grips as to why Miranda would purposely lie about me and have me fired. This was my livelihood.

I had just moved there eight months ago. Now I had to pack up and head home to my mother's in Milledgeville, a fourteen-hour drive. I had nowhere else to go. I made it to my mother's home in Milledgeville just in time for Thanksgiving.

I did all that I knew how to do: fight this. I took it all the way up through the chain of command by letter, requesting appeals all the way to the Supreme Court. The government has its own attorneys that fight for them, but I had no one fighting for me. I contacted an attorney, but could not afford one. Each letter received from the courts stated that my case had nothing to do with judicial or bipartisan issues. I was denied, denied, and denied.

I kept telling them that it had nothing to do with judicial or bipartisan issues but wrongful termination, plain and simple. All I could do was give up. I wrote to the White House, and they replied, stating that my case was being reviewed elsewhere, so no luck there. I wrote my congressional representative and the Equal Employment Opportunity Commission. I was just SOL (shit out of luck) at this point. I told the courts that I wanted my job back in another location, and of course, I would like compensation for all the pay lost. I had hit a brick wall. I had no help and was out of resources. The government won, but I did not lose, not completely and not right away.

God opened another door for me.

One year later, I was offered a position within a different agency I had applied to. Now I was heading to Saxton.

Being lied on and lied about can turn a person's life upside down. People should really think before they purposely hurt another for their own gain, and that includes me too. I wanted justice for the wrong done to me, but because I could not get it, it haunted me. It made me angry. I wanted to call Miranda and ask her why. I knew it was all a lie, but I could not prove it, and no one wanted to look into my story.

I have no faith in the justice system.

Petite Breaux

~Sixteen~
WHERE IS THE LOVE?

Wallace had been acting weird lately. I thought he was going through a midlife crisis. He had been coming across as unhappy and distant. I did not know what to say. I got the feeling that he was not happy with the relationship. I knew he was not happy, and I had confronted him on it more than once. Everything I said yes to, he said no. He was always contradicting me. When we first met, I thought we were good for one another. We were very compatible. We had so many things in common but were so different. We had different attitudes about life. His attitude was better. He was more laid-back, settled, and knew how to budget. I was a "do what I have to do to survive and worry about the rest later" type. Lately...*hmm, scratch that*...For several years, he had been acting weird.

    Things had just been the opposite. We could not get on the same page. I wanted to love him as I did in the beginning, but things were changing. The distance growing between us was taking a toll on me. We had been apart too long. I decided, after continuous apartment renting and the annual increase in rental cost, to purchase a home.

    Wallace was helpful before the move and after. Wallace said if I needed him to co-sign, that he would. I had already told myself that if I need a co-signer that I would not buy the house. He had his own home in another state, so it was time for me to own my own. I appreciated his offer.

    I was glad he was there for me and wanted to help if needed, but like I have said plenty of times, there is nothing like having your own.

    Things were still very odd with Wallace, and I knew his underlying issue was me. I was just not that girl anymore. I was not loving or affectionate enough, and my underlying question to myself was, *Why not?*

    I guess I was changing. I knew he had changed. Wallace even said, "When we first got together, you tried too hard too fast."

    Well, it wasn't quite exactly like that, but I did try, and I fell hard for him fast, after letting down my guard.

    "You're too extreme, and now, you're not wife material," he said

    According to him, I didn't do anything for him. In fact, I didn't do anything but sit on my hands;

I didn't cook, and all I did in the bedroom was sleep. He knew I didn't cook when he met me. He wanted to do all the cooking. I did cook, but it was rare.

"I quit my job not once, but twice to be where you were, no questions asked," I said.

"What is that supposed to mean? What exactly was it you gave up?"

"What did I give up? Are you serious?"

"I will not say it again. If you are unhappy, you need to find someone who makes you happy, because I am good."

Every weekend we had the pettiest of arguments, and I did not want to argue anymore. I had no tears, no emotions for it any longer. I had conserved all my emotions. I cried more while watching movies. We had been together way too long to continue this way. Everything I said he found something at fault with it.

Making casual conversation, I said I was adventurous and that he was the safe one in the relationship. He was the levelheaded one and I was the impatient one. We balanced one another out.

"Do you think being adventurous is harmful to a relationship or a marriage?" he asked.

I said no. It is not as if I am jumping off bridges or putting us in harm's way. If I had not mentioned this, he would have never raised the question. We were discussing televisions for the house.

"Best Bargains has a sale, with twenty-four month financing," I said.

"No, we're not using any credit. We were trying to decrease your debt. Do you have the money

Petite Breaux

in your purse? Sure, buy it, but no financing. How long would it take you to save for it?"

"Too long," I said.

He took his usual phrase out. "We will talk about it later."

When he came down the next weekend, I said, "I wanted to stop in at Best Bargains," so we did.

Out of respect for our relationship, I tried to include him by asking, "Do you want to get the TV?"

"No." Just a flat-out no.

"Are you telling me 'no' like I am your child? You are not my daddy," I said.

"No, but I am telling you, you are not getting the TV."

Am I being punked in here and don't know it? I thought to myself.

"What if something goes wrong with your car? You're not thinking about the long haul."

"I can't think about what might happen tomorrow," I said. "I am living day by day, one day at a time, and I just want to live and be happy. I don't do anything for myself. I don't shop. I have been paying bills, and that's all." Bottom line, Wallace gave me an ultimatum when I said I was getting the TV.

"If you get the TV, I am leaving."

"Leaving? Leaving the store or what? You not going on the cruise?"

"If you get the television, this relationship between you and I is over."

"Really? You're giving me an ultimatum? That is not fair of you to do this to me. I would never give you an ultimatum. That is not right, and Lord knows, I could have given you plenty. Okay, I am getting the TV, and you can leave. I work every day and some overtime when needed. I should be able to buy myself something that I want. Last time I looked, my last name was not yours." I wasn't trying to humiliate him with that, but we were not married.

We had been together for fifteen years, and every time I mentioned marriage, there was another excuse or another flaw he found with me. If Wallace and I were to stay on this path with our relationship, I would believe that it was for a reason, because too many seasons had come and gone.

Wallace and I have taught each other much in our time and years spent together. He has taught me how to love again, has opened my heart to trust again, how to budget, how to cut back on spending, how credit is debt and it is better to spend cash whenever possible.

I want to believe that I have opened his heart to love and family commitment, taking vacations, spending quality time together. We have together taught each other respect, loyalty, trust, and compromise.

I fell in love with Wallace. He has much wisdom; he is very smart and uses his brain. We treat each other with respect. Wallace is an awesome person, one in a million, or, as I call him, a different breed of a man. One thing I do not want to do is undo it all. Don't get me wrong. He is there for me, no matter what, and he loves me. We have shared just as many great times as bad. We have done as much, or more, in our time together as most married couples.

Every time I moved to another state, who was there to take the trip to help me move? Wallace! I love him, too, but sometimes I question our love for one another. Are we still in love with each other?

I believe it is the distance pushing me away in the past. Family interference and the years that we spent apart in different states definitely was reason with our dysfunctional relationship.

We have been living more apart than together. You would think once we got the chance to spend time together, we would be inseparable, but nope, not so. We bicker over the pettiest things, and it draws a wedge between us.

Most of the time I believe this is my entire fault. Wallace and I lost our compassion for one another down the road, but the loss was especially mine.

I never wanted to be with another man, but sometimes I thought that maybe I needed to be with someone else. I feel we can get this back.

We used to go out to restaurants, not for dinner, but just to have a piece of pie, a cup of coffee, and a conversation. We used to stay in, rent a movie, and just cuddle up on the couch. We used to take bubble baths and have our glass of wine.

Those days have been gone for years now, and I ask myself, *Why can't I just give him what he needs to make him happy in this relationship?*

This man has been there for me for every surgery and sickness that I have had.

But, he has always had issues with me, and I really did not have any issues with him. To me, most of it was petty.

I was torn. I wanted to be there sometimes, and sometimes I did not. I just did not know.

There was a lot of deep digging. I felt guilty because of my mixed emotions.

Maybe we were both to blame.

We each had stopped putting our best foot forward to keep the relationship going. I know I got on his nerves, and he got on mine as well. It was nothing serious. It was all petty, and his good outweighed his bad on any given day. I can truly say that it's not him; it's me.

Petite Breaux

~ Conclusion ~

Sometimes I feel as if all the bad in my life has outweighed the good. One thing I did not do was give up. I am still standing, and the fight is still in me! My past is gone. It is other events and people that have come and gone in my life, but they are not worth mentioning, not worth the attention, nor the paper to write it on. I cannot change a thing that has happened in my life, and I do not sit around dwelling on it.

I have forgiven all involved, including myself. Can it be forgotten? *Hmmm*, probably not. I just try to stay away from those who have no good intentions. I stay away from negativity, drama, arguing and chaos as much as possible.

Everything I have experienced in life has made me a much better person. I have survived, and my life is still moving forward. That girl is no more. Those ways are no more. I was harming not only myself but my family, too. I had to make a change. I had to change. I have changed.

I just want to be happy, take a vacation every now and again, and live a simple and comfortable life.

Still, I sometimes have those feelings from my younger years about my looks. The concerns I experienced before about my nose, my ears being too big, and now the marks of my childbearing years, are no longer an issue. I know that I would never spend the money to fix my so-called imperfections or ever be able to maintain it, so I decided to be happy in the skin that I am in. Changing those problem areas will not change who I am as a person. Just be me.

I don't have much, but what I do have is mine. I want more for myself and I am still trying to get there. I don't know exactly what it is that I want to do, but I don't want to just remain idle.

I need to find something that makes me happy. I need to be happy so that those around me can be happy. I don't want pettiness, but I do want to do bold and new things. My life was nothing nice for a long while. Now I can breathe somewhat easier. I am just sick and tired of all the drama, I have had enough!

My children and I have come a long way in life together. We grew up together and we are very close. We are not where we need to be, but we know that we love each other and will always be there for one another.

Cecilia now has questions of the past about Christian: why did I stay, why didn't I leave him? Cecilia has some underlying hurt from everything that has happened, but she lives on her own and is doing well, but I feel that all that has happened keeps her leery of relationships.

Melik has three children. He spent a few years in the Army, which I thought would help his anger issues, but it only made them worse. He is very protective of his family and his children. He suffers from PTSD, and now he is just coping with life.

Sharmayne does not bite her nails any longer; she too has somewhat of relationship issues after all that she had to endure growing up. She has taken some college courses, focusing on life and doing well.

My mother still lives on her own in a different state, but she is in good health and she visits every year.

I believe my family and I could probably use family counseling, but I know none of them would agree.

I have helped my family so much recently that I cannot help myself at times; now, I have decided that I cannot help as much as I did before.

I am no better than the next person. I have the same issues, more or less, as others.

Not all of your business has to be displayed for the world to view.

I just want to be better than I was the day before. I used to be a doer, but I would do without thinking things through. If I wanted it done, it had to be now. Now I think too much. I think long and hard over things, but I am still somewhat of a doer, I am just better at it.

I have a few pet peeves, such as I cringe when things are out of place. I don't like it when a chair is not pushed to the table. I cannot stand a toilet seat left up or unmade beds, and I don't care for much company. I am content being home alone enjoying a good movie.

I went back to school later in life because I wanted a career, a trade, not just a job anymore. Although I achieved my master's degree, I did not achieve the position that I had hoped for. You can get the degrees, but with no experience in the field, it is hard to gain the position that you majored in. Another thing I gained from attending college is a big ass student loan bill I am stuck paying.

I am very grateful to be employed, but do I like my position? No. I feel like I am at a dead end and the job is mentally exhausting.

I still live as if there is no one else around, just to remind myself of independence. I don't want to have to depend on anyone to take care of me or pay my bills. I am independent but also interdependent.

Wallace and I will be okay. We can work this through. Some may not agree with my decision. Some will talk. Everybody talks; that is what people do. They talk if you are doing well. They talk if you are doing badly.

I now have a bucket list is to visit Africa, Hawaii, Alaska, Paris, England, and Italy. I want to go see an Opera and a live Broadway show.

I want to purchase my own RV. I have already done kayaking and parasailing; now I just need to zip line, learn to ride a motorcycle, and take swimming lessons—for the fourth time.

Life is moving along in the right direction. Although hurt, angry, slightly bruised, and a little broken, I was determined not to let my past haunt me, so I continue to move forward in life.

A friend said to me, thank God we don't look like what we been through.

REMEBER as long as you are breathing, it's never too late to start over again.

My life choices did not break me!

Made in the USA
Charleston, SC
24 December 2015